4 95

C78 - 869

TEACHING LITERATURE TO ADOLESCEN   SHORT STORIES

STEPHEN DUNNING
University of Michigan

TEACHING
LITERATURE
TO
ADOLESCENTS

SCOTT, FORESMAN AND COMPANY

The author wishes to thank those who have given permission to reprint the following:
An excerpt reprinted from the story "A Man for Mom" in December 1964 *True Romance*. An excerpt from"A Ride into Town" by Berton Roueché in *The New Yorker*, XL, No. 27 (August 22, 1964). "After You, My Dear Alphonse" reprinted with permission of Farrar, Straus & Giroux, Inc. and Brandt and Brandt from *The Lottery* by Shirley Jackson. Copyright 1943, 1949 by Shirley Jackson. "Appointment with Love." Reprinted from Collier's Magazine. Copyright 1943 by Crowell, Collier. Permission to reprint granted through author's agent, August Lenniger Literary Agency, New York. "The Chaser" from *Fancies and Goodnights*. Copyright 1940 by John Collier. Reprinted by permission of Harold Matson Co., Inc. An excerpt from **A Handbook to Literature** by Thrail, Hibbard, and Holman, copyright 1960 by The Odyssey Press, Inc. "Jacob" from *The Plainsmen*. Copyright © 1956 by Jack Schaefer. Reprinted by permission of the publisher, Houghton Mifflin Company. "The Landlady" copyright © 1959 by Roald Dahl. This story first appeared in *The New Yorker*. Reprinted by permission of Alfred A. Knopf, Inc. and Laurence Pollinger Limited from *Kiss, Kiss* by Roald Dahl. An excerpt reprinted from the story "Nightmare Wife" in December 1964 *True Romance*. "Peanuts" cartoon © United Feature Syndicate, Inc. 1956. Reprinted by permission. "The Princess and the Tin Box" copyright © 1948 James Thurber. From *The Beast in Me and Other Animals*, published by Harcourt, Brace & World, New York. Originally printed in *The New Yorker*. And from *Vintage Thurber* by James Thurber, copyright © 1963 Hamish Hamilton, London. An excerpt from "Raymond" by Emily Hahn in *The New Yorker*, XL, No. 27 (August 22, 1964). An excerpt from "The Secret Life of Walter Mitty" copyright © 1952 James Thurber. From "The Secret Life of Walter Mitty" in *My World—and Welcome To It*, published by Harcourt, Brace & World, New York. Originally printed in *The New Yorker*. And from *Vintage Thurber* by James Thurber, copyright © 1963 Hamish Hamilton, London. Excerpt from "Stranger in Town" by Nadine Gordimer, copyright © 1964 by Harper's Magazine, Inc. Reprinted from the November, 1964 issue of *Harper's Magazine*. **Stubby Pringle's Christmas** copyright © 1964 by Houghton Mifflin Company. Reprinted by permission of the publisher. "Taste" copyright, 1951 by Roald Dahl. This story first appeared in *The New Yorker*. Reprinted by permission of Alfred A. Knopf, Inc. and Laurence Pollinger Limited from *Someone Like You* by Roald Dahl. Excerpt reprinted from the story"Was I Driving This Child Insane?" in December 1964 *True Story*.
Thanks also go to the following publishers for permission to reproduce their pages:
The Literary Review and Henry Kreisel for sample page of "Broken Globe" by Henry Kreisel in *The Best American Short Stories 1966*, from *The Literary Review*. Sample page from *More Junior Authors* reprinted by permission of The H. W. Wilson Company. Copyright © 1963 by the H. W. Wilson Company. Sample pages from *Readers' Guide to Periodical Literature* and *Short Story Index Supplement* reprinted by permission of The H. W. Wilson Company. Sample pages from *Subject and Title Index to Short Stories* reprinted by permission of The American Library Association.

Preface

Teaching Literature to Adolescents: Short Stories is intended to help teachers-to-be at the undergraduate level and teachers of some experience improve their teaching performance.

Part One contains four principles which can be applied concretely to the teaching of short stories. Actual stories, embedded in the text, to be read and worked on, provide evidence and support for these principles. I hope not all the stories are ones you already know; and when I refer to other stories such as Ring Lardner's "Haircut" and James Thurber's "The Secret Life of Walter Mitty," I count on your remembering them, and, should you be properly provoked, on your rereading them.

Parts Two and Three are surely the highlights of the book. In them, Jack Schaefer and Roald Dahl talk about teaching stories and comment on stories of their own. I am sincerely grateful to these authors and hope the prose of my making that surrounds their contributions will not embarrass them.

Part Four explores what is perhaps the most complicated part of our teaching task—approaches to the short story. Again, actual stories are used as examples for exercises in taste, style, and structure. Part Five explores the library resources that we know about, vaguely, but may have forgotten.

The short story, rich enough, of appropriate length, and somehow naturally interesting to students, is a unique vehicle for our teaching performance. We teachers should expect, with just a hint of arrogance, that our own good performances will be emulated by our students. If we perform well, it will be because we were well prepared for our teaching (although we will sometimes bungle) and because we are honest in our judgments and reactions (although we will often be uncertain). But even as star performers we must insist that our students get into the act. If taking the time to involve students means that we fail to cover the entire course of study, we can rest content in the knowledge that students will improve as readers by our performance and their involvement with it.

I owe substantial thanks to Lee Bernd, who designed Part Five, and to Charles Brashers, Leroy Haley, and Marion Laetz for feeding me ideas, ordering my prose, and stimulating my sometimes flagging energies. Curt Johnson, freelancer and editor of *December* magazine, and Carol Embury at Scott, Foresman have proved the fastest blue-pencils west of Ann Arbor. But, as is always the case, the author is stuck with the faults that remain despite all aid and comfort.

Stephen Dunning
Ann Arbor, Michigan
June, 1968

Contents

PART ONE

The Teaching of Short Stories

As E. M. Forster suggests, an interest in discovering "how things turn out" in a story is characteristic of all men. Indeed, one great advantage to teaching short stories is that students find the short story the most approachable and satisfying of all literary forms. From fables, from "once-upon-a-time" fairy tales, from their parents' bedtime inventions for them, young people have learned, intuitively, much about narrative structure—about beginning, middle, and end. Before TV, they read stories at home for pure enjoyment, but as TV pre-empted "quiet time," offering narrative in easy-to-open packages, short stories in print became things to be studied in school rather than enjoyed at home.

Fortunately for the teacher, TV doesn't provide—and gives no promise of providing—all it is capable of, and this fact provides a second advantage in teaching short stories. Young people (and even some old folks past eighteen) are vaguely dissatisfied with the pap of most TV narrative, uneasy with the good-guys-win adventure tale, the boy-wins-loses-wins-girl romance, and the formula success epic. True, many current stories in print share with TV drama a predictable narrative line, and most examples of both offer characters so thin that the stereotype is quickly identified, and quickly forgotten. And, also true, most "stories" in print and on TV guarantee freedom from genuine intellectual or moral complications, thus providing easy escape from the hard work of thinking. But students have discovered that at least *some* stories-in-print are better than most stories-on-tube. One of man's intellectual imperatives is, apparently, that time-passers don't satisfy over the long haul. Because it rarely rises to provocation and complexity, TV is not the enemy.

Print itself has its advantages. Hunches about characters and inferences about their motives can be checked out in print; the TV narrative, on the other hand, flickers and disappears. The printed short story keeps the reader aware of everything that is going on, permits him to go back and forth in the text for evidence. Since it *can* be scrutinized readily, a printed story almost has to be better, more artful, than its TV counterpart. The artful story in print invites the reader to assume the feelings, voices, and postures of narrator and characters; the story on the tube—by the nature of its medium— invites the viewer to disengage. The reader's pleasure is different (and superior) to the viewer's.

The short story's third virtue is its length. Despite the numerous schemes invented for breaking the five-classes-per-week schedule, the great majority of schools still devote five weekly periods, rang- ing from thirty- to seventy-minute "hours," to English. Aspects of a short story can be introduced and considered, and conclusions can be drawn within the hour. Students can take ground on narrative, character, or conflict. If a teacher selects for teaching a short story that sours in a particular class (a story too complex, too subtle, or too silly; one which because of setting, characterization, or subject is unengaging to young readers), he pays a relatively slight penalty: one class period. Assume, on the other hand, he has committed him- self to a novel or play. Unable to change plans gracefully when that longer work proves unsuitable, he may forfeit weeks.

A fourth reason why short stories prove useful in the curriculum is that they fit all major kinds of teaching units. Of course, the genre (or types) unit allows the grouping of short stories so that character- istics of the genre illuminate the reading of individual stories. But thematic units such as "Survival" or "Initiation" may also begin from theme-setting short stories. Such topical units as the junior- high "Heroes of the Frontier" utilize short stories and fictionalized "true adventure." Even the chronological survey provides a home for short fiction unless the end of the school year comes before the survey reaches "the modern era." Units based on traditions (Ro- manticism, Naturalism), on modes (the comic, the ironic), and on major literary figures (Hawthorne, Poe) may feature the short story.

A fifth advantage in teaching short stories is that they provide a unique laboratory for consideration of many aspects of all literature. Although there are singular skills involved in reading poetry, drama, nonfiction, and longer fiction, the short story permits us to teach skills useful in reading all other forms as well. The claim that the short story differs from the novel mainly in length is of course not wholly accurate, yet one can learn qualities of irony from De Maupassant's "The Necklace" just as readily—more readily in fact—as from John Barth's *Giles Goat-Boy.* Stories by James Joyce, D. H. Lawrence, and Eudora Welty are structurally so subtle and linguistically so complex that they may be talked about in poetic terms. The structure of the plotted short story (a conflict established and met at a point of crisis) and its method of proceeding (usually description and narration laced with dialogue) are congenial to young readers. And since short stories as a genre pose fewer problems than other genres, since the power and appeal of narrative tend to lessen the pain of close reading, young people will learn much about all forms of literature from studying the short story.

These reasons for teaching short stories can be illustrated. Consider the following story.

After You, My Dear Alphonse

Shirley Jackson

Mrs. Wilson was just taking the gingerbread out of the oven when she heard Johnny outside talking to someone.

"Johnny," she called, "you're late. Come in and get your lunch."

"Just a minute, Mother," Johnny said. "After you, my dear Alphonse."

5 "After *you*, my dear Alphonse," another voice said.

"No, after *you*, my dear Alphonse," Johnny said.

Mrs. Wilson opened the door. "Johnny," she said, "you come in this minute and get your lunch. You can play after you've eaten."

Johnny came in after her, slowly. "Mother," he said, "I brought Boyd
10 home for lunch with me."

"Boyd?" Mrs. Wilson thought for a moment. "I don't believe I've met Boyd. Bring him in, dear, since you've invited him. Lunch is ready."

"Boyd!" Johnny yelled. "Hey, Boyd, come on in!"

"I'm coming. Just got to unload this stuff."

15 "Well, hurry, or my mother'll be sore."

"Johnny, that's not very polite to either your friend or your mother," Mrs. Wilson said. "Come sit down, Boyd."

As she turned to show Boyd where to sit, she saw he was a Negro boy, smaller than Johnny but about the same age. His arms were loaded with
20 split kindling wood. "Where'll I put this stuff, Johnny?" he asked.

Mrs. Wilson turned to Johnny. "Johnny," she said, "what did you make Boyd do? What is that wood?"

"Dead Japanese," Johnny said mildly. "We stand them in the ground and run over them with tanks."

"How do you do, Mrs. Wilson?" Boyd said.   25

"How do you do, Boyd? You shouldn't let Johnny make you carry all that wood. Sit down now and eat lunch, both of you."

"Why shouldn't he carry the wood, Mother? It's his wood. We got it at his place."

"Johnny," Mrs. Wilson said, "go on and eat your lunch."   30

"Sure," Johnny said. He held out the dish of scrambled eggs to Boyd. "After you, my dear Alphonse."

"After *you*, my dear Alphonse," Boyd said.

"After *you*, my dear Alphonse," Johnny said. They began to giggle.

"Are you hungry, Boyd?" Mrs. Wilson asked.   35

"Yes, Mrs. Wilson."

"Well, don't you let Johnny stop you. He always fusses about eating, so you just see that you get a good lunch. There's plenty of food here for you to have all you want."

"Thank you, Mrs. Wilson."   40

"Come on, Alphonse," Johnny said. He pushed half the scrambled eggs on to Boyd's plate. Boyd watched while Mrs. Wilson put a dish of stewed tomatoes beside his plate.

"Boyd don't eat tomatoes, do you, Boyd?" Johnny said.

"*Doesn't* eat tomatoes, Johnny. And just because you don't like them,   45
don't say that about Boyd. Boyd will eat *anything*."

"Bet he won't," Johnny said, attacking his scrambled eggs.

"Boyd wants to grow up and be a big strong man so he can work hard," Mrs. Wilson said. "I'll bet Boyd's father eats stewed tomatoes."

"My father eats anything he wants to," Boyd said.   50

"So does mine," Johnny said. "Sometimes he doesn't eat hardly anything. He's a little guy, though. Wouldn't hurt a flea."

"Mine's a little guy, too," Boyd said.

"I'll bet he's strong, though," Mrs. Wilson said. She hesitated. "Does he . . . work?"   55

"Sure," Johnny said. "Boyd's father works in a factory."

"There, you see?" Mrs. Wilson said. "And he certainly has to be strong to do that—all that lifting and carrying at a factory."

"Boyd's father doesn't have to," Johnny said. "He's a foreman."

Mrs. Wilson felt defeated. "What does your mother do, Boyd?"   60

"My mother?" Boyd was surprised. "She takes care of us kids."

"Oh. She doesn't work then?"

"Why should she?" Johnny said through a mouthful of eggs. "You don't work."

"You really don't want any stewed tomatoes, Boyd?"   65

"No, thank you, Mrs. Wilson," Boyd said.

"No, thank you, Mrs. Wilson, no, thank you, Mrs. Wilson, no, thank you, Mrs. Wilson," Johnny said. "Boyd's sister's going to work, though. She's going to be a teacher."

70 "That's a very fine attitude for her to have, Boyd." Mrs. Wilson restrained an impulse to pat Boyd on the head. "I imagine you're all very proud of her?"

"I guess so," Boyd said.

"What about all your other brothers and sisters? I guess all of you want
75 to make just as much of yourselves as you can."

"There's only me and Jean," Boyd said. "I don't know yet what I want to be when I grow up."

"We're going to be tank drivers, Boyd and me," Johnny said. "Zoom." Mrs. Wilson caught Boyd's glass of milk as Johnny's napkin ring, suddenly
80 transformed into a tank, plowed heavily across the table.

"Look, Johnny," Boyd said. "Here's a foxhole. I'm shooting at you."

Mrs. Wilson, with the speed born of long experience, took the gingerbread off the shelf and placed it carefully between the tank and the foxhole.

"Now eat as much as you want to, Boyd," she said. "I want to see you
85 get filled up."

"Boyd eats a lot, but not as much as I do," Johnny said. "I'm bigger than he is."

"You're not much bigger," Boyd said. "I can beat you running."

Mrs. Wilson took a deep breath. "Boyd," she said. Both boys turned to
90 her. "Boyd, Johnny has some suits that are a little too small for him, and a winter coat. It's not new, of course, but there's lots of wear in it still. And I have a few dresses that your mother or sister could probably use. Your mother can make them over into lots of things for all of you, and I'd be very happy to give them to you. Suppose before you leave I make up a big bundle
95 and then you and Johnny can take it over to your mother right away . . ." Her voice trailed off as she saw Boyd's puzzled expression.

"But I have plenty of clothes, thank you," he said. "And I don't think my mother knows how to sew very well, and anyway I guess we buy about everything we need. Thank you very much, though."

100   "We don't have time to carry that old stuff around, Mother," Johnny said. "We got to play tanks with the kids today."

Mrs. Wilson lifted the plate of gingerbread off the table as Boyd was about to take another piece. "There are many little boys like you, Boyd, who would be very grateful for the clothes someone was kind enough to give
105 them."

"Boyd will take them if you want him to, Mother," Johnny said.

"I didn't mean to make you mad, Mrs. Wilson," Boyd said.

"Don't think I'm angry, Boyd. I'm just disappointed in you, that's all. Now let's not say anything more about it."

110   She began clearing the plates off the table, and Johnny took Boyd's hand and pulled him to the door. "'Bye, Mother," Johnny said. Boyd stood for a minute, staring at Mrs. Wilson's back.

"After you, my dear Alphonse," Johnny said, holding the door open.

"Is your mother still mad?" Mrs. Wilson heard Boyd ask in a low voice.

115   "I don't know," Johnny said. "She's screwy sometimes."

"So's mine," Boyd said. He hesitated. "After *you*, my dear Alphonse."

Does this story support our reasons for teaching short stories? Well, as a story that satisfies the natural interest in narrative, "After You, My Dear Alphonse" is only modestly successful. Three characters are talking and doing; but the things they say and do may seem pointless to many readers. However, students can be interested in the fact that the story isn't predictable, doesn't resolve itself as do most TV stories. No happy ending here. ("No ending at all," some students will complain.) But when narrative seems to fail because it is not resolved, students can be diverted to other concerns.

For example, even senior-high students will find Jackson's story complex enough to warrant discussion and thought. Indeed the psychological action requires attention *because* not much happens on the physical-action level. Rich enough to stand scrutiny during class (and rereading after class), "After You, My Dear Alphonse"—because it is told almost wholly through simple dialogue—must be read below its surface.

The story is short enough that within a class period certain aspects can be carefully considered by seventh-graders of average ability; older students can of course dig more deeply.

The story will fit into a variety of units:

A. A ninth-grade types or genre unit; for example, "An Introduction to Short Stories." ("After You, My Dear Alphonse" contrasts neatly with a heavily plotted short story.)

B. An eleventh-grade chronological survey of American Literature.

C. A narrower chronology; for example, "Recent Prose Stylists."

D. A unit featuring representative contemporaries; for example, a tenth-grade unit on Thurber, Jackson, and Bradbury.

E. A focus on Jackson alone; comparison of "After You, My Dear Alphonse" with "The Lottery."

F. A junior-high topical unit: "Negro Characters in Fiction."

G. A senior-high thematic unit: "Innocence" (or "Initiation"), "Brotherhood" (or "Prejudice"). (Focus here might be on Mrs. Wilson's "corruption" as opposed to the "innocence" of Johnny and Boyd.)

Because short stories "have always been there" and are "easy to teach," teachers may be overconfident in approaching them. Characteristically, however, teachers do not take full advantage of the genre. They tend to teach the stories of Poe with the same read-then-ask-and-discuss procedures that they use with the science fiction of Ray Bradbury. They deal with ephemeral sports stories and problemless teen-age problem stories in just the same way that they approach the morally significant fiction of Melville. They tend to settle for what happens in a story when what is of signal interest is how a writer has made it happen. Analyzing how Shirley Jackson has arranged meaning in "After You, My Dear Alphonse" can be of genuine intellectual interest; in any case, it is of more interest than synopsizing the incident involving a Mrs. Wilson and two little boys.

Considering four principles for teaching short stories may help us to teach them better.

Principle one: A teacher should limit his aims in teaching any one story. Too often, teachers load onto a single story everything they know about the genre. This excess results more from poor planning than from innate malevolence: teachers often neglect to focus and limit their aims. Generally, teachers should spend only a period or two on one story. The energy, say, of "The Secret Life of Walter Mitty" is insufficient for a week's work. What might be accomplished with it, then? In a class period or two, students might deal with the imagery Thurber uses and with the specific devices that trigger Mitty's heroic daydreams; they cannot cover all stylistic, structural, characterizational, and thematic aspects at once.

All well and good. But there is chance of lapsing into error in this regard for, in a sense, the English major who is teaching literature has learned too much. He has learned to watch for symbol and allusion, to sense the pattern of imagery that gives unity to a story. He notes connotation and the purposeful rhythmic patterns of a story. Such structural devices as foreshadowing and flashback reveal themselves to him as he reads and considers techniques of pacing and plot.

Having learned to "experience" fully the stories of James and Mansfield, or Chekhov and Salinger, the young teacher attempts his first teaching assignment. The ninth-grade anthology offers him some standard but relatively simple fare along with a dozen inconsequential stories in there as interest-arousers. And the young teacher innocently heaps onto the first assigned story, whether a "standard" or an inconsequential filler, the aggregate wisdom of his college career.

After a week's work with such a teacher, the ninth-grader's dinner-table report might be: "We've been studying short stories," or "We've been reading 'The Secret Life of Walter Mitty.' It was pretty interesting, for a while."

Two years later, wise in the ways of teaching, our former innocent has learned the value of focus in teaching. He has paired two stories, for purposes of contrast, and has emphasized two or three things in his teaching. From this accomplished teacher's class, a student might report: "We've been studying point of view and characterization in stories by Schaefer and Jessamyn West." And if pressed, our student paragon might further explain how the points of view in the two stories are different, even say why the difference makes a difference.

Preparing a story for teaching might well consist of three preliminary steps. First, the teacher reads and rereads a story until he has mastered it. Second, he lists points that the story makes and the literary aspects it demonstrates. Third, he brings to bear his knowledge of the class to which he will teach the story and prepares to concentrate on those points and aspects that fit the particular class.

A good short story is rich enough for study at a variety of levels and within a variety of contexts. The teacher's key instructional task is to establish some priorities, to focus on particular aspects of reading fiction that will help his students emerge from the workshop of the story as improved readers.

Please recall (or even reread) Jackson's "After You, My Dear Alphonse" (pp. 3–5). Among many workshop possibilities for it, two warrant priority for teaching. The first is understanding the *connotation.* The second, relevant to the reading of most serious imaginative literature, is understanding the *theme.* Either subject would provide an adequate focus for teaching, providing it were appropriate for a particular class.

What Jackson connotes or implies in "After You, My Dear Alphonse" is more significant than what she denotes or makes explicit. Understanding the connotations or implications of the story is a part of what is often called "between-the-lines reading."[1]

PEANUTS ®   **By Schulz**

1. *Between-the-lines reading* may indeed be an unfortunate term. When I first heard it, as a student in junior high school, I thought that wonderful things were writ invisible in the spaces between the printed lines. Does the term not connote to students a magic available to teacher-wizards but generally withheld from mortal students? On the other hand, terms like *close reading* seem to deny that there's anything more to literature than what can be seen, pointed to, and mouthed. Another puzzlement to live with.

Reading between the lines is required by a parody in *Mad* magazine in spite of that magazine's directness and visualizations; it is also required of students who will deal successfully with the metaphor and tone in any complex poem. Close reading of Jackson's story is necessary, too. But in order to provide ninth-graders with useful practice in understanding connotation, questions must be exact and carefully arranged:

> What might Mrs. Wilson be thinking about when she asks "What did you make Boyd do?" (p. 3, l. 21)

> Why do you think Mrs. Wilson says "You shouldn't let Johnny make you carry all that wood"? (p. 4, l. 26)

> What beliefs about Negroes does Mrs. Wilson reveal when she says, "There's plenty of food for you to have all you want"? (p. 4, l. 38)

> What are the obvious and the subtle echoes of "*Doesn't* eat tomatoes, Johnny. And just because you don't like them, don't say that about Boyd. Boyd will eat *anything*." (p. 4, l. 45)

The teacher should also be ready to identify places in the story where what is left unsaid is more significant than what is said:

> "Boyd wants to grow up and be a big strong man so he can work hard," Mrs. Wilson said. "I'll bet Boyd's father eats stewed tomatoes." (p. 4, l. 48)

> "I'll bet he's strong, though," Mrs. Wilson said. She hesitated. "Does he . . . work?" (p. 4, l. 54)

and

> ". . . She's going to be a teacher."
> "That's a very fine attitude for her to have, Boyd." Mrs. Wilson restrained an impulse to pat Boyd on the head. "I imagine you're all very proud of her?" (p. 4, l. 69)

Part of the teacher's planning job is to arrange some of the connotative lines from simple to complex. For example, students will more readily see what's implied by Mrs. Wilson's gossipy interest in Boyd's family situation than they will understand the implications of her "disappointment" (p. 5, l. 108). They will understand Mrs. Wilson's pique and removal of the gingerbread (p. 5, l. 102) more readily than her benevolence as she puts the gingerbread between the boys (p. 5, l. 82).

The dramatic tension, the conflict of "After You, My Dear Alphonse," exists in its connotations. If a young reader identifies to the point of picking up some of the social implications, he has "read between" at least some of the lines. Mature readers may be asked to consider the connotations of the images—" [Boyd's] arms were loaded with split kindling wood" (p. 3, l. 19), and "Suppose before you leave I make up a big bundle and then you and Johnny . . ." (p. 5, l. 94). Such images connote slavery.

The most mature reader might discover that although it is explicit that Boyd is a Negro (p. 3, l. 18), it is *not* explicit that the Wilsons are white. Few readers of any age will come to that question and, in truth, the question is fancier than it is important. But raising it can lead to talk about how the reader's experience affects his reading of fiction.

Getting to the theme of "After You, My Dear Alphonse," to the "essential experience" (or to what some of my students call the "nitty gritty") may be more difficult than understanding the connotations of the story. The term *villanelle* has a dictionary meaning that is precise and useful; students can learn the word, use it, and be understood. But a handbook or dictionary definition for *theme* is not likely to be as easily understood. To build students' experience with the term, even to distinguish *theme* from *plot,* simple lessons are necessary. Here an eighth-grade class is working toward a sense of theme:

TEACHER. Well, Paula, what's the point or the basic idea of the story?

PAULA *(Whose thoughts, characteristically, are elsewhere).* There isn't much action. It's sort of a scene with these two boys getting lunch from one boy's mother. The guest is a Negro, and he and the boy who lives in the house keep saying this dumb thing about Alphonse . . .

TEACHER. Whoa, Paula. You're telling what happens. Are you telling me the point of the story? The idea behind what happens?

PAULA *(Frowns.)*

TEACHER. Well, has the point of the story to do with *lunch?*

PAULA. No.

TEACHER. Has it to do with Alphonse?

PAULA. No. That's the dumb thing the kids keep saying.

MARTIN. I think the point is that the mother is trying to help the Negro kid but doesn't know how. And she shouldn't be trying anyway.

MAX. She'd be doing the right things if Boyd needed help, but he doesn't.

TEACHER. I wonder.

MAX. I mean she was trying to be kind because she had all these ideas about Boyd's family.

TEACHER. Well, I think that's closer to the point or theme.

MARY ANN. The point is that the mother's stupid. Prejudiced. The kids aren't.

TEACHER. I thought Paula said the story was about two boys having lunch.

PAULA. That *is* what it's about, but lunch isn't the point. Lunch isn't the theme.

TEACHER. Could a story *about* two boys having lunch have a theme, say, of brotherhood? *(Class allows it.)* Could a story about baseball have the theme of—what?

SAL. One baseball story, "Flashing Spikes," has the theme of courage. *(Teacher beams.)* You see, there's this guy, a second baseman who used to play for the Chicago White Sox, only they called them the Black Sox because there was this big scandal . . .

TEACHER. *(Teacher sighs, reaches for the spelling book.)*

However fuzzy, such discussion is probably sharper than most discussion in most eighth-grade classes. If theme is the statement of general significance that emerges from a story, the theme of "After You, My Dear Alphonse" might be that the society Mrs. Wilson represents is corrupt, that what the boys represent is innocent. But it is not important, at first, that students learn the story has the theme, say, of corruption. Certainly talk about theme should not be limited to an exercise wherein students guess the magic word fitting the slot: The theme is _____. Students should be encouraged to discuss whatever thematic possibilities come out of their reading: In the Jackson story, prejudice, brotherhood, insensitivity. The good teacher turns back into the text for support or denial of such possibilities, for there will be relevant and irrelevant responses, real possibilities and extratextual oversimplifications.

A precise statement of theme in "After You, My Dear Alphonse" —and in most stories—is hard to come by; but it is crucial that students have the experience of groping for it. A sense of the abstraction, the theme, may eventually emerge. If theme is the intrinsic general significance lying behind a story of particular people in a particular situation, analysis of these people and their situation will promote the generalization. Shirley Jackson doesn't drop a moral tag into her story saying that the young are innocent, the old corrupt, but this idea will come out. Mrs. Wilson's "screwiness" displays stereotypical thinking characteristic of middle-class (middle-age) life. Confronted by an individual who doesn't conform to her notions, and especially since she feels she is acting generously, Mrs. Wilson is resentful and acts foolishly. The boys' actions are plain, innocent fun.

The situation that Jackson has observed (or imagined) and recognized makes a comment to all readers who know anything about America of the past fifty years. The thematic echoes are inescapable. We believe in Mrs. Wilson, whose story this is, since she confirms our sense of plausibility. We know other Mrs. Wilsons. As readers, we are finally sorry for her; we are pleased that the boys are free of her particular "screwiness."

In focusing instruction, the idea is to see that appropriate aspects of a story are emphasized and others excluded. Those we decide to treat are treated thoroughly rather than superficially. Of course, however sharp the plan for focus, no teacher will be able to rule out additional questions and opinions that excited students will bring into discussion. But planning for focus will make it a little easier to swing back to central issues, will work against haphazard discussion in class, and will reflect a plan built on priorities. When discussion is good, the aspects we select for teaching will be related to what we cannot possibly teach all at once: the whole story. But in order for this to happen, the teacher must—initially—limit his aims.

Principle two: In teaching, the focus must be on the text of the story. In Principle one, two priority aims, understanding of connotation and theme, were used to demonstrate the limiting of aims in teaching a story. Determining priority aims means finding the points of intersection among students' backgrounds, what a particular story offers, and the capabilities the teacher brings to his reading of a story; this is essential preparation for teaching. Once in the classroom, the teacher's essential necessity is—of course and obviously—keeping the text of the story in front of students.

Of course and obviously, but my experience, corroborated through discussion with others who regularly sit in on classes, is that the text is literally set aside during many discussions ostensibly concerned with what or how a story means. In one class dealing with De Maupassant's "The Necklace," I observed thirty long minutes devoted to chalkboard diagrams which purportedly represented the form of the short story and featured definitions of "rising action" and ("Get this down in your notes!") *denouement;* in another class I gave ear to an introductory lecture on the local colorists, anticipating discussion of Bret Harte's "The Outcasts of Poker Flat"; in an "average" ninth-grade class, I witnessed presentation of the tradition of Naturalism, made graphic through a kaleidoscopic peek at paintings from the "Ash Can School," the entire performance preparatory to discussion of Jack London's "To Build a Fire"; in a twelfth-grade honors section I learned to distinguish the traditional plotted story (on chalkboard: "people in a situation which is complicated to the point of climax, then resolved") from the modern story (on chalkboard: "the telling 'slice of life,' the situation revealed, then intensified, but unresolved") as preliminary to reading a story by Chekhov. In an infinite variety of classes, I saw an inexhaustible assortment of introductory exercises designed to illuminate the story to be read but actually postponing, in some instances indefinitely, the difficult business of looking at the text.

The common failure of such preparatory operation is that the teaching procedures were deductive; that is, teachers started from generalizations that particular stories were to demonstrate. Stories became data for exemplifying generalizations about form, "schools," or traditions.

Learning occurs best inductively, from the observation of instances that lead to a generalization. The term "inductive" teaching has become a shibboleth. But in the educational literature wherein its virtues are consistently praised, it is demonstrated less often than it is pronounced. Even though the term verges on cliché, the process it describes has not been widely practiced (or experimented with and found wanting): the process, like "accommodation of individual differences," has been praised as theory and ignored in practice.

Having students discover something through examples requires artful teaching. First, the teacher must formulate a precise, worthy idea. (This step, a *deductive* procedure capitalizing on the teacher's expertise, is necessary even though the give-and-take of discussion will modify and sometimes even deny the idea.) Once the idea is formulated, the examples must be found and ordered: What parts of the text will you stop on? Which example will you consider first? In the classroom, timing is of the essence: When is the best moment to move from instances to generalizations about style? How many examples of irony should be provided before generalization is appropriate? How often must students feel the implications of first-person short stories before a thesis about that point of view will have reality? How many instances of the traditional plotted story should students experience before they are asked to describe its characteristics?

To put this point another way, we need to provide students with some of the textual experience we have acquired over the years. Our students need practice in doing what we have learned to do, and the only way students can get the practice they need is to rummage around in the text. If we decide that students need know something about *mood,* we go to where mood exists. Here are two sentences from the first paragraph of Poe's "The Fall of the House of Usher":

> During the whole of a dull, dark, and soundless day in the autumn of the year, when the clouds hung oppressively low in the heavens, I had been passing alone, on horseback, through a singularly dreary tract of country; and at length found myself, as the shades of the evening drew on, within view of the melancholy House of Usher. . . . I looked upon the scene before me —upon the mere house, and the simple landscape features of the domain—upon the bleak walls—upon the vacant eye-like windows—upon a few rank sedges—and upon a few white trunks of decayed trees—with an utter depression of soul which I can compare to no earthly sensation more properly than to the afterdream of the reveller upon opium—the bitter lapse into every-day life—the hideous dropping off of the veil.

I would want to discuss the diction, the sentence lengths and rhythms, and, perhaps, the assonance of the passage before asking the question of mood: What feeling or mood do these sentences create? Hoping to demonstrate the nature of humor that comes from innocence or naïveté, with Max Shulman's doughty Dobie Gillis in front of us, we go into the laboratory and find Dobie in a characteristic imbroglio:

> "What a magnificent portrait!" I cried, racing to a painting that hung over the mantel.
> "Sir Joshua Reynolds," said Mrs. Willet.
> "Excellent likeness," I declared. "Excellent!"
> "Sir Joshua Reynolds is the one who painted it," said Mrs. Willet, casting me a curious look.
> "I *will* have my little joke," I replied, giggling wildly. "But now I must see the dining room."[2]

2. Max Shulman. *The Many Loves of Dobie Gillis* (New York: Bantam Books, Inc., 1964), p. 171.

Dobie is as ignorant of how to behave as he is of the identity of Sir Joshua Reynolds.

I restate my belief in the inductive process and then say, hurriedly, that induction is both difficult to arrange and readily susceptible to failure. Arranging data for discovery is harder than making pronouncements and then asking students to find supporting instances. And there is, in almost every lesson, a time for telling. If you have prepared a lesson showing how point of view makes a difference, if you have arranged and presented examples so that most students discover, say, the effect of varying reactions to a single event, you must sometimes name the game for your recalcitrants: "Well, it is clear to some of us that while Mrs. Wilson sees her offer of a bundle of clothes as a generous offer, Boyd sees it as silly."

In most classes there are too many excursions from the text and there is too little physical involvement with it—eyes and mind on print, fingers pointing to words and lines, mouths reading sentences aloud. This is not to say there is a conspiracy afoot to keep students from their rightful textual inheritance. Rather, teachers tend to avoid the text because it is easier to generalize than to particularize. Moreover, teachers are motivated by goodness. The folklore of goodness says that teachers must relate the literature they teach to the lives of the youngsters they teach. "Have you ever seen an adult with a mask on?" we ask, readying eleventh-graders for Hawthorne's "The Minister's Black Veil." "How many have been to a street fair or a bazaar?" we ask, anticipating a wide-range discussion of Joyce's "Araby" for our advanced placement seniors. Perhaps instead we should ask students to look so hard at a work of art that *they* can relate to *it.*

One technique for keeping the text in focus is to require students to prepare plot summaries as preparation for discussion. These summaries should be written out so that students can read them aloud if called on. Occasionally, they should be prepared to be handed in and graded. Although the idea of summarizing plots may connote the sterility of book reporting practices to some, turn-of-the century pedagogy to others, the nonsense of one-volume compedia to yet others (*Themes, Summaries, and Characters of the World's 100 Best Short Stories*), the writing of plot summaries encourages students to read carefully.[3] It is logical for a teacher to insist that students read a story before discussing it in class, and a required plot summary will make the story stick.[4]

---

3. This is a better activity for "traditional" than for the "modern" short stories, but I proceed in the belief that even with the latter you may sometimes sit in class surrounded by bountiful discussion of Chekhov's view of life when what you want to know is what happens, either actually or symbolically, in his misty "Dreams."

4. "Read the story?" I heard one colleague respond to another's question. "I haven't even taught it yet."

Before they can comprehend the *mood* of a description or a narrator's tone in dealing disdainfully or warmly with his characters,
students need an understanding of the literal narrative as a base to
work from. If the story is complex, the who's-doing-what-where is
primary: even in the most homogeneous of classes, a story rich
enough to challenge the best reader will float right by the less able
readers.

Inexperienced teachers may resist assigning plot summaries,
even though it becomes clear that some students haven't made even
tentative contact with an assigned story. "Won't this be an awful
bore for the student who *can* read?"

Risk it—at least for the time. Insist on summaries until students
show that they have little trouble preparing them. So long as students'
papers and oral responses show that they didn't "get" the story at
its narrative level, requiring summaries might be—perhaps should
be—standard procedure. Good and average students will find summaries useful for grander excursions into motive, character, symbol,
or irony. For the best students there will be confirmations and occasional insights.

Having students prepare summaries will discourage the clutter
of spontaneous vagueness: "In 'The Necklace' this woman is real
pretty and she likes jewelry and stuff like that, but she doesn't have
a very rich family and can't get anybody to marry her, except this
clerk from the Department of Health, Education, and Welfare and
she is miserable because she wants to have a lot of expensive stuff
and really live it up . . ." and so on.

As students' summaries improve with practice in writing them,
additional preliminary-to-discussion assignments will keep them on
appropriate paths. Assume that an important aspect of De Maupassant's "The Necklace" is its situational irony. Before discussing
"situational irony," students write out narrative summaries in their
notebooks. In addition to this firm requirement, you offer optional
questions. One is about motive: "Why was Mme. Loisel unwilling
to admit she'd lost the necklace?" Or you may offer a question requiring the student to stand, temporarily, with one or another de-
batable response: "Is it Mme. Loisel's pride or the nature of her
society that keeps her from admitting the loss?" (Black-and-white
questions often produce good grey answers.) Any tenth-grader who
can read and summarize "The Necklace" can offer an opinion on
either question; the polarized question might require rereading for
evidence. Both the summary and the optional questions will encourage discussion, good discussion. If you want to go beyond
situational irony in class discussion, consider with students the
effects of the ironic situation on the main characters.

An option to the read-then-summarize assignment is the in-class preview. The preview is especially appropriate before assigning the reading of complex stories. A tenth-grade class assigned the reading of Stephen Vincent Benét's "By the Waters of Babylon" may need help getting the narrative straight. The journey itself is basically chronological although interrupted by cryptic references (Ou-dis-sun for the Hudson River, Ashing for Washington), a death song (sung by the narrator), the narrator's long dream (a vision of the destruction of New York City), and occasional asides and flashbacks. These interruptions alone would slow some readers and stop others, but the style of the first-person narration will be even more troublesome. Here, in a relatively easy paragraph that comes close to the explicit statement of theme, the narrator is reporting what he saw:

> I told and [my father] listened. After that, I wished to tell all the people but he showed me otherwise. He said, "Truth is a hard deer to hunt. If you eat too much truth at once, you may die of the truth. It was not idly that our fathers forbade the Dead Places." He was right—it is better the truth should come little by little. I have learned that, being a priest. Perhaps, in the old days, they ate knowledge too fast.[5]

Some sections, especially those where the narrator is exploring the devastated city, are easy to follow; others, especially those preceding the journey, will confuse many readers. But the story is eminently worth reading and teaching. For such a story in which *how* the story happens is as important as *what* happens, your own oral summary might help students get through the *what*, to the *how*. The trick is to tell enough to facilitate reading but not so much as to destroy all reason for persevering. For example:

> Benét's "By the Waters of Babylon" describes a journey of a young man of the Hill People, a people of the future yet far more primitive than our own. The young man burns for knowledge about the desolate Place of the Gods. The proposed journey is reluctantly approved by his father, a priest of the Hill People. The young man sets out and encounters omens, wild animals, hostile forest people, and a treacherous river. Successfully reaching the dangerous Place of the Gods, he sleeps for the night in a "tower" remaining intact after the Great Burning and Destruction. He has a dream in which he at once sees and comprehends how the city "newyork," once a hive of activity and light, was

---

5. *Selected Works of Stephen Vincent Benét* (New York: Holt, Rinehart & Winston, Inc., 1942), p. 175.

virtually destroyed in what we assume was an atomic raid. He realizes that this was a city not of gods, but of men.

If such a summary would facilitate reading, discussion after reading could involve students directly with problems of text. The qualities of character of the narrator might be compared and contrasted with the character of the narrator's father or with the men of the extinct civilization. The concrete and figurative images the narrator uses evoke a sense of primitive nature: the wind is "the voice of the gods as they flew through the air"; his own spirit is "a cool stone"; a ceremonial chant is "like the buzzing of bees in [his] head"; the great river is "like a giant in the sun"; he has "a fire in his bowels . . . [and] mind"; his heart is "cold as a frog"; and he feels "naked as a new-hatched bird." A hard look at such figures could lead to useful, meaningful generalizations about tone. Checking the textual evidence for an understanding of theme could be interesting—and useful.

Preparing summaries encourages, but doesn't guarantee, basic understanding. Through them, chances improve that discussion will be pointed rather than haphazard, because significant literary aspects are often rooted in the narrative. In the case of the irony of Mme. Loisel's situation, understanding depends upon a knowledge of the setting; the setting established Mme. Loisel's pride in relation to the society she aspires to: the setting actually creates the point of the story.

Any student who can read "The Necklace" can summarize it; his problem during discussion is often that he hasn't read it. The making of summaries encourages reading. Moreover, for good students, writing outline sentences will be a fixing exercise providing the basic context from which more sophisticated issues will emerge. For the less astute student, summarizing "The Necklace" will give him the chance to glean from class discussion of motivation or irony some sense of what those terms mean. The literal-minded student who has prepared a summary may be able to keep more fanciful classmates from wildly extravagant flights.

In lieu of a summary, reading aloud the first sixteen paragraphs of "By the Waters of Babylon" would set the reader up for the journey that follows. The puzzling proper names (for example, *Ubtreas* and *Ashing*), remnants of the extinct civilization, might cause unwarranted confusion unless they are explained before they are encountered in reading.

More often, however, students will discover (and enjoy discovering) a story's meaning independently. Indeed, sometimes simply alerting a good class to the fact that a story presents puzzling difficulties will challenge them to solve those difficulties voluntarily. Other times a preview will supply explicit hints for solving key difficulties: explaining[6] the "Alphonse and Gaston" comic strip, letting students in on the extravagant caricature of courtesy that the phrase "After You, My Dear Alphonse" conveys, will be useful in some cases.

The hope behind such efforts is that they will lead to class discussion which will produce useful learning. The best seed for fruitful discussion is your own set of prepared questions. Carefully thought through and carefully cast questions are the best single preparation for good discussion. You need not be a slave to the "logical" order in which the questions are asked, but keeping them sharp and answerable is crucial. Students who get only vague notions of a story through independent reading can, by patient teaching, be brought to a threshold from which they step into meaningful discussion.

Principle three: In getting students to extend beyond narrative level, the sequence should be from concrete to abstract, from text to extra-textual. Limiting aims (thus improving chances that skills of reading literature are taught thoroughly), and focusing upon text (making sure students deal with what is on the page) are the two primary principles in teaching short stories to adolescents. The third principle is in some ways an elaboration of the first two. The key difference is this: our ultimate aim is extension of students' skills as readers rather than consolidation of their skills as readers of simple narrative. We hope to develop virtuosity in students. We want to give students enough experience in approaching fiction from various perspectives to ensure that such abstractions as "point of view" and "Naturalism" are tools for understanding rather than fuzzily understood tags.

Many students will be doing well to practice and master the reading of fiction at its literal narrative level. For such students, we will have improved the odds that they will get their money's worth from magazine subscriptions, will read with greater pleasure while waiting turns in beauty shops and dentists' offices. But there are also many students who will not settle for the literal level. Students who show an ability to cut quickly to the narrative core of a story are ready for instruction in approaching fiction at other levels.

---

6. Or, perhaps, showing. For one source see Thomas Craven's *Cartoon Cavalcade* (New York: Simon & Schuster, Inc.).

One such level is *structural*. Structure is a more comprehensive term than plot. Structure encloses plot and deals with the general management of the story, with the arrangements of points of view, with how flashback and foreshadowing cut into straight chronology.

Another such level is the *rhetorical,* which has to do with the sound system of fiction—language and style. We consider the tone of a line as spoken by a character, the relationships and distance among characters or between narrator and character; we seek a sense of a story's moods and feelings; we develop awareness of how rhythm, diction, and metaphor achieve them. We consider the assumptions an author asks us to make about the fictional situation he is managing and about the characters he puts into it.

The *symbolic* level deals with the echoes of meaning beyond that insisted upon by the narrative; we confront image and other non-literal phenomena; we consider the story's theme. Serious short stories have symbolic implications that make fictional lives significant to real lives.

The *contextual* level of fiction is different from the others in that its emphasis is outside of the single work. More exactly, context here refers to the setting in which a particular work lies, rather than the meaning a single work establishes for itself. Understanding context means seeing a given work in larger frameworks: other works by the same author, works of similar theme or content by different writers, works of other types coming from a particular milieu. Context may derive from the character of a genre, from a literary tradition, and from knowledge of the society it re-creates or from which it was written.

Although the divisions between such levels can become blurred (for example, arrangements of point of view might be considered *structural,* while their effects might be considered *rhetorical),* the four above seem useful in placing appropriate emphasis on different ways the *how* of a story is accomplished.

Contact with the how of fiction is contact with fiction's art. Plain narrative is not artless, but it is limited in its art. When students are ready for complexity, when they are beyond the point of being satisfied by narrative alone, we must be ready to show them that special fun that persuaded us into the profession in the first place. *Finally* we can talk ideas, probe symbolic and metaphoric levels, look at the rhetoric of one story, investigate the points of view of another. Once the threshold of literal understanding has been crossed by our students, we no longer need concern ourselves very much with keeping the story straight, with helping students remember which character did what to whom. We are ready to do what we've been trained to do.

In our joy, our first error is in assuming that adolescent students are as worldly as we. Forgetting Mrs. Wilson and the two boys, refreshed by our college notes on James' "situation revealed" tag for plotless stories, we plunge into the *structural* features of "After You, My Dear Alphonse." We turn to the meaning of the story through *rhetorical* analysis of relative distances between Mrs. Wilson and each of the two boys. Touching lightly on such symbols of the adolescent culture as haircuts and class rings, we explain that there are both universal and particular symbols in literature and suggest that students find examples in "After You, My Dear Alphonse." We establish *context* for the story by citing the Watts riots (which occurred when our students were in elementary school!). We use labels representing our own experience in the erroneous assumption that the experience is shared by our students. Again, we deduce rather than induce.

Among the important axioms of labeling is that useful generalization depends upon myriad instances. Moreover, few simple instances serve as perfect examples of generalization. The abstract label of Naturalism connotes a formative, deterministic Nature and hapless individuals in it. If we begin with the abstraction and then read Jack London's "To Build a Fire" as a demonstration of Naturalism, we might reasonably expect the victim in the story to be a pawn of Nature, a puppet who cannot possibly escape freezing to death in the frozen Yukon. After all, London *was* a Naturalist, wasn't he?

Our reading of the story unsettles us. London makes it clear that his protagonist's death comes from arrogance. The "old-timer on Sulphur Creek" had offered the advice he should have heeded: "No man must travel alone in the Klondike after fifty below." The protagonist's destiny is determined once he willfully launches himself alone into the seventy-five-below-zero wasteland. At a point when he could yet return to safety, he gets a sign that it is too cold to continue:

> He spat again. And again, in the air, before it could fall to the snow, the spittle crackled. He knew that at fifty below spittle crackled on the snow, but this spittle had crackled in the air. Undoubtedly it was colder than fifty below—how much colder he did not know. But the temperature did not matter. He was bound for the old claim on the left fork of Henderson Creek, where the boys were already.

Yet continue he does, alone, deliberate—arrogant.

Similarly, abstractions about the rhetorical qualities of fiction are unlikely to benefit students who haven't dealt with basic rhetorical elements. With rhetorical analysis very much in vogue today, with many teachers coming into the profession full of good notions about "the authorial stance," ready with ways to assess the "distance" between characters and with notions of "persona," students are hearing a great many abstractions about the rhetoric of fiction. Rhetorical analysis is undeniably one of the most exciting and productive kinds of analysis; the question is not whether students should learn about it but, rather, how its abstraction can be reduced.

A good tenth-grade class can readily cover the literal ground of Ring Lardner's "Haircut." A barber tells a newcomer to town about one Jim Kendall. Jim was a great practical joker and the barber reveals the quality of Jim's wit through a dozen anecdotes. For example, "sore" that his wife had gone to his employers trying to get some of Jim's wages to buy food for their family, Jim makes up his mind to "get even." A circus is advertised and Jim

> told his wife and two kiddies that he was goin' to take them. . . . [H]e would get tickets and meet them outside the entrance to the tent.
>
> Well, he didn't have no intentions of bein' there or buyin' tickets or nothin'. He got full of gin and laid round Wright's poolroom all day. His wife and the kids waited and waited and of course he didn't show up. His wife didn't have a dime with her, or nowhere else, I guess. So she finally had to tell the kids it was all off and they cried like they wasn't never goin' to stop.

On the literal level, the story seems almost plotless. We learn in the second paragraph that Jim Kendall is a practical joker who got killed. The continuing narrative is a string of episodes detailing Jim's jokes; they require, in the telling, about as much time as a haircut. We learn that Jim died accidently on a hunting trip, but we aren't sure exactly how or why.

It is at the structural and rhetorical levels that the story becomes richer and more complex. The point of view from which the story is told provides some thought-provoking interplay. We realize that we view Jim and all other characters through a particular kind of narrator, one whose sensibilities are dulled. The plain facts of Jim's jokes are peculiarly unfunny; the narrator unwittingly shows Jim to be unbelievably rotten to his wife and children, a lecher willing to risk force to get what he wants from women, an unreliable employee who gets fired from the one good job he has held, a heavy drinker, a joker oblivious to the painful consequences of his jokes. He seems, in short, the complete heel.

Even on first reading, students will note Jim Kendall's coarse insensitivity and the fact that he just isn't funny. What is out of balance is the fact that the narrator, the barber, repeatedly sings Jim's praises as a joker. There is a vast ironic distance between the virtues the narrator claims for Jim and what is revealed through the incidents narrated.

The narrator's point of view is not very revealing unless considered along with its rhetorical implications. Jim and the narrator are soulmates of like sensibility. To the narrator, Jim "certainly is a card" no matter how gross his behavior. Even though one of Jim's grislier jokes is turned on the narrator, causing him both discomfort and expense, the narrator sings an admiring refrain: "He certainly was a card!" Jim Kendall is the doer, the narrator an approving spectator. The narrator admires Jim so much he even emulates him in speech. Jim's witty nickname for Paul, a brain-damaged boy, is "the cuckoo." Jim sends Paul out for left-handed monkey wrenches ("Of course," the narrator confides, "they ain't no such thing as a left-handed monkey wrench") and for a key to the pitcher's box before a baseball game. ("They wasn't nothin' in the way of gags that Jim couldn't think up, when he put his mind to it.") Eventually the narrator slips into calling Paul "the cuckoo" without first giving his idol credit for the original flash of wit.

Once the reader sees the close kinship between narrator and protagonist, sees how everything Jim does is filtered through the narrator, the near-plotless story takes form. The narrator isn't smart enough to see that the pattern of incidents he relates adds up to a clear case of (justifiable) homicide. He buries in his anecdotes the fact that Paul, "the cuckoo" who kills Jim on the hunting trip, "was gettin' better, that they was times when he was as bright and sensible as anybody else." The reader tuned into the narrator's kinship with Jim (and sensing the rhetorical pattern of the separate incidents) has no doubts. Paul killed Jim. We learn "what happened" *in spite of* the narrator. We know why Paul killed Jim because we have come to despise him as Paul did.

Observing the pattern of the jokes Jim played, aligning the character of the narrator with Jim, assessing the effects of Jim's jokes on others, a plotless string of incidents becomes a neat tale of homicide raising a genuine moral issue. Murder rather than accidental death lies at its climax.

Tenth-graders will need to understand the character of the narrator before they will feel Jim Kendall's inhumanity or be able to decide whether Jim deserved what he got. They should read passages aloud, repeating until the narrator's tone of voice is approximated:

> I guess he run pretty wild durin' the time he was on the road
> for them Carterville people, and besides that, he'd had a couple
> little affairs of the heart right here in town. As I say, his wife
> could of divorced him, only she couldn't.

Reading aloud and then discussing the intended effect of key passages is a start toward understanding the rhetoric of "Haircut."

We want to develop in our students the power of abstraction, of generalization. We hope they will be able to apply general ideas to the reading they will do independently. We are not interested in making them into encyclopedias of particulars. It is not our ultimate aim that students understand connotation only in "After You, My Dear Alphonse" nor that they see the significance of the narrator as character only in "Haircut." But such particulars, practiced and rehearsed, allow generalization to develop.

A generalization about the recurring character types inhabiting Lardner's fictional world, for example, might emerge from a survey of three or four of his stories. Once a variety of small-town rednecks and two-bit city drummers have been paraded, a generalization can be made about Lardner's characters, their attitudes and manners of behavior. The generalization "transfers." Encountering a "Lardner-type character" in independent reading may provide a reader with a recognition that will bring real pleasure.

Let's consider this idea of extension from the concrete to the abstract through one additional example. A rereading of the first paragraph of "Rip Van Winkle" will demonstrate both the concrete base for abstraction and the possibility of extending this base through the teacher's skillful reading.

> Whoever has made a voyage up the Hudson must remember
> the Kaatskill mountains. They are a dismembered branch of
> the great Appalachian family, and are seen away to the west
> of the river, swelling up to a noble height, and lording it over
> the surrounding country. Every change of season, every change
> of weather, indeed, every hour of the day produces some change
> in the magical hues and shapes of these mountains; and they are
> regarded by all the good wives, far and near, as perfect barom-
> eters. When the weather is fair and settled, they are clothed
> in blue and purple, and print their bold outlines on the clear
> evening sky; but sometimes, when the rest of the landscape is

cloudless, they will gather a hood of gray vapors about their summits, which, in the last rays of the setting sun, will glow and light up like a crown of glory.[7]

Irving's scene-setting will strike most young readers as pretty much of a drag. Why doesn't Irving simply say that the story is set in the Hudson River Valley among the Kaatskills? This first paragraph surely doesn't key the reader into the action. What's Irving's purpose in proceeding as he does? Was he padding out a skimpy story line? Was he being paid by the line?

The difference between concretion and abstraction is something like this: Abstractly, we might say that the function of the first paragraph is to "set the scene." You can tell students this and hope that they will accept "scene-setting" as a thing writers do. Then on with the story. Concretely, and conversely, you might investigate *how* the piece works. *Is* there too much description here?

The rhetorical purposes of the paragraph are achieved in the diction. We help students find the pattern of words and phrases that describe the mountains: *noble height, lording, magical, purple, crown of glory.* What calculated effect lies behind such diction? Students will discover this to be a "regal" or "majestic" diction. The mountains are kings, wearing the colors of royalty. If there are villages (and we don't yet know that there are), they would be in postures of humility at the feet of the mountains. There is the hint of magic; prospects of enchantment come to mind; we even expect a happy ending from such a setting.

Although we get no inkling of precisely *what* is going to occur, we do sense *how* it will occur. Although the first paragraph is excessive so far as the action of the story is concerned, it is indispensable to the rhetorical level. We know that the lordly mountains, those "barometers," shape and predict life. Both the actual and psychological scenes are set. Irving has put us in "tone of mind" that grants him his pretense of credibility. Our disbelief is suspended.

The text we have read closely shows how the author wants us to proceed as readers. We are ready for enchantment, for magic. For confirmation of our rhetorical set we turn to Irving's preface to "Rip Van Winkle" as it appeared in the *Sketchbook.* (Students accept the duplicated copies we provide, awed by our scholarship and thoroughness; we are delighted to be able to distribute out-of-copyright materials.) Our question, before students read, is "Who wrote this story about 'Rip Van Winkle'?" Here's the preface:

7. Mary and Wallace Stegner, *Great American Short Stories* (New York: Dell Publishing Co., Inc., 1957), p. 33.

A Posthumous Writing of Diedrich Knickerbocker

The following tale was found among the papers of the late Diedrich Knickerbocker, an old gentleman of New York, who was very curious in the Dutch history of the province and the manners of the descendants from its primitive settlers. His historical researches, however, did not lie so much among books as among men; for the former are lamentably scanty on his favorite topics, whereas he found the old burghers, and still more their wives, rich in that legendary lore so invaluable to true history. Whenever, therefore, he happened upon a genuine Dutch family, snugly shut up in its low-roofed farmhouse under a spreading sycamore, he looked upon it as a little clasped volume of black-letter, and studied it with the zeal of a bookworm.

The result of all these researches was a history of the province during the reign of the Dutch governors, which he published some years since. There have been various opinions as to the literary character of his work, and, to tell the truth, it is not a whit better than it should be. Its chief merit is its scrupulous accuracy, which indeed was a little questioned on its first appearance, but has since been completely established; and it is now admitted into all historical collections as a book of unquestionable authority.

The old gentleman died shortly after the publication of his work, and now that he is dead and gone, it cannot do much harm to his memory to say that his time might have been much better employed in weightier labors. He, however, was apt to ride his hobby his own way; and though it did now and then kick up the dust a little in the eyes of his neighbors, and grieve the spirit of some friends for whom he felt the truest deference and affection, yet his errors and follies are remembered "more in sorrow than in anger," and it begins to be suspected that he never intended to injure or offend. But, however his memory may be appreciated by critics, it is still held dear by many folk whose good opinion is well worth having; particularly by certain biscuit-bakers, who have gone so far as to imprint his likeness on their New Year cakes, and have thus given him a chance for immortality almost equal to the being stamped on a Waterloo medal or a Queen Anne's farthing.[8]

8. *ibid.*, pp. 31-32.

Have we only complicated matters? Have we confused the question of authorship instead of confirming what we learned from the opening paragraph of "Rip Van Winkle"? Who wrote this story, anyway?

The factual answer is that "'Rip Van Winkle' was written by Washington Irving, American author, story writer, essayist, historian biographer, born in 1783 and died in 1859." The more useful answer, the rhetorical answer, is that the author was Diedrich Knickerbocker, now deceased, an eccentric historian who read history from life rather than from ancient books and who, despite his peculiarities, produced historical records generally accepted as authentic and precise. Instead of asking students to accept this "fact" innocently, you guide them toward the rhetorical intent. If they will accept Knickerbocker as the author, for rhetorical purposes, there is a new character in the story: the narrator himself. Now, reading that the Kaatskills are a "dismembered branch of the great Appalachian family," are "seen away to the west of the river, swelling up to a noble height," you assume that for Knickerbocker such information is necessary to his performance as historian. Through his editor, one Washington Irving, Knickerbocker presents facts that are compelling both because they are true and because they are revealed by a character who has a distinctive personality of his own.

Now we have access to the narrator's personality as he reveals himself as well as the "factual" file from Washington Irving, who presents Knickerbocker to us. We learn from Irving what Knickerbocker prized in scholarship, are offered a wry insight into the quality of Knickerbocker's writing, and then an immediate support for Knickerbocker's reliability as historian.

A look at the epigraph (written on the chalkboard if not provided with the text of the story) will reveal something more of our author-historian:

By Woden, God of Saxons,
From whence comes Wensday, that is Wodensday.
Truth is a thing that ever I will keep
Unto thylke day in which i Creepe into
My sepulchre—

Cartwright[9]

The epigraph tells us again that the author wants us to accept his honesty, his truthfulness; it also suggests the author's interest in

9. *ibid.*, p. 33.

the antiquarian *(thylke, Creepe)*. Having suspended our disbelief, granting Irving his epigraph joke, we are ready for further revelation of the historian, Knickerbocker—a man of consummate integrity! Even the epigraph he selects pledges truth unto death.

In moving from concrete to more abstract matters, we will often assist students' understanding through external, out-of-text information that is genuinely relevant. What is genuinely relevant and what is "window dressing" is a nice question, but generally what is relevant is what immediately enlarges the students' consideration of text. Thus the diction and the scene-setting of the first paragraph of "Rip" are illuminated both by the prefatory matter and by the epigraph to the story. We might in some cases go on to look at the "Note" and "Postscript" which follow the story.

In considering the rhetorical aspects of the introductory paragraph, extratextual data may be appropriate. (In going to the prefatory matter and the epigraph, however, we have actually stayed within the literary context of the story. As Irving wrote the story for publication, and as it was first printed, this material was included.) We will often operate on the structural, rhetorical, symbolic, and contextual levels of analysis, but our extensions should be rooted in the text. There must be time in the English class to look closely, to hear, to follow the ways an author puts words together. After such investment, students will show some of the control over abstraction that characterizes artful reading. A survey of early American literary history, a rehearsal of Irving's biography, or an investigation into the authenticity of the epigraph will not push them forward in the reading of a story—this particular story, at least. We must take from such extratextual possibilities only those that will erase shadows in the text we are looking at.

Principle four: The quality of a short story should be approached as a genuine issue.[10] Even as an abstraction, quality is perplexing: What *is* good? What bad? Making judgments regarding quality in fiction is further complicated because it involves the reader's taste. We know what we like—*each* of us. It is through the print on the page that useful discussion of taste (and of quality) is partly manageable.

One of the long-term aims for the literature program must be to move the seventh-grader from "I like that" or "I didn't like that" responses toward text-based responses. The fumbling responses of the seventh-grader (who also knows very well what *he* likes) show

---

10. The material in principle four appeared, in slightly different form, in the *English Journal,* May 1968. Reprinted by permission of the National Council of Teachers of English.

that the scope of his liking, his sense of "appreciation," is under-developed. His prerequisites for a good story are an interesting sub-ject, a fast pace, and a happy ending. Our aim is to refine his liking or disliking. By the time he is a tenth-grader, our student should be sounding like this: "I like the ways Irving shows that Rip isn't to be taken seriously. Look, for example, . . ."

Improving student taste, then, should be one of the teacher's chief aims in the literature curriculum. Along with helping the stu-dent improve his skills in reading literature, along with providing him some access to the pleasure that literature can bring, refining the student's sensibility of what is "good" and "bad" (that is, pro-moting him toward discriminating reading) is a prime goal.

But we too seldom teach literature as though its quality were an honest issue. We hear ourselves saying, "You're going to like this story by Lardner." Or "Within the limits he sets for himself, O. Henry is a master . . . ." Or "This is a fine example of Poe's use of setting as psychological background . . . ." Textbooks aid and abet us by touting selections in the language of the pitchman. ("Here's a masterpiece of suspense" begins a headnote in one popular anthol-ogy.) Good stories will make their own claims. We teachers should be promoting consideration of the particulars that lie behind the student's "I like this" or "I don't like that." We should exercise our expertise in directing the student's attention to things he might not discover himself.

Having students offer a *because* or having them deal with *why* is the first step in developing their literary taste. The serious adult reader finds pleasure in the structure of a piece of fiction, in its lin-guistic richness, in the complex of aspects that, taken together, urge him to re-create its experience. When the teacher asks seventh-grader Franklin what it was he liked about the hero, when he asks eighth-grader Frances why "what happened" seems "nice" to her, those young readers are headed toward higher satisfactions—if they can begin to answer.

Teachers can help improve taste by refusing students' easy answers and by pushing students to their own dissatisfactions. This implies moving from generalities to specifics. The move from "I like the ending" to "The ending seems to me possible and believable" is a small but certain step toward particularization. Creating addi-tional dissatisfactions (with implausible dialogue, or stock characters, or an excess of coincidence, or a faulty linking of events) will help the uncritical reader improve his sense of good fiction.

Young readers like to have things work out happily. They don't mind the spilling of blood, but the blood had better be the bad guy's or the nasty wolverine's or the hero surrogate's rather than the hero's or heroine's. Students must be weaned from sweet illusions that life's problems always work out happily. Through literature they can be reminded that there are real problems in the real world they themselves inhabit. Not all problems disappear with the dispatch that the writers of fiction for the *Ladies Home Journal* and *Good Housekeeping* arrange.

Below is an inductive technique that will suggest a way of involving students in questions of taste. A ninth-grade class trying the exercise will surely be provoked into an exchange of opinions. Some consideration of what constitutes good fiction is almost inevitable.

Let me pose a readily answerable question: Which of the two stories following do *you* like better? A harder question, now: Why do you prefer it? An even harder question may provoke a different answer: Which is the superior story? In what ways is it superior?

It may comfort you in answering these questions to know that both stories first appeared in reputable American magazines, and that both were discovered by anthologizers and reprinted in a variety of collections. Both, then, have virtues enough that editors of some experience and taste selected them for high school audiences. Here are "Appointment with Love" and "The Chaser."

Appointment with Love

S. I. Kishor

Six minutes to six, said the great round clock over the information booth in Grand Central Station. The tall young Army lieutenant who had just come from the direction of the tracks lifted his sunburned face, and his eyes narrowed to note the exact time. His heart was pounding with a beat that shocked him because he could not control it. In six minutes, he would see 5 the woman who had filled such a special place in his life for the past thirteen months, the woman he had never seen, yet whose written words had been with him and sustained him unfailingly.

He placed himself as close as he could to the information booth, just beyond the ring of people besieging the clerks. . . . 10

Lieutenant Blandford remembered one night in particular, the worst of the fighting, when his plane had been caught in the midst of a pack of Zeros. He had seen the grinning face of one of the enemy pilots.

In one of his letters, he had confessed to her that he often felt fear, and only a few days before this battle, he had received her answer: "Of course 15

you fear . . . all brave men do. Didn't King David know fear? That's why
he wrote the Twenty-third Psalm. Next time you doubt yourself, I want you
to hear my voice reciting to you: 'Yea, though I walk through the valley of
the shadow of death, I shall fear no evil, for Thou art with me' . . ." And he
20 had remembered; he had heard her imagined voice, and it had renewed his
strength and skill.

Now he was going to hear her real voice. Four minutes to six. His face
grew sharp.

Under the immense, starred roof, people were walking fast, like threads
25 of color being woven into a gray web. A girl passed close to him, and Lieutenant Blandford started. She was wearing a red flower in her suit lapel,
but it was a crimson sweet pea, not the little red rose they had agreed upon.
Besides, this girl was too young, about eighteen, whereas Hollis Meynell
had frankly told him she was thirty. "Well, what of it?" he had answered.
30 "I'm thirty-two." He was twenty-nine.

His mind went back to that book—the book the Lord Himself must
have put into his hands out of the hundreds of Army library books sent to
the Florida training camp. *Of Human Bondage,* it was; and throughout the
book were notes in a woman's writing. He had always hated that writing-
35 in habit, but these remarks were different. He had never believed that a
woman could see into a man's heart so tenderly, so understandingly. Her
name was on the bookplate: Hollis Meynell. He had got hold of a New York
City telephone book and found her address. He had written, she had answered. Next day he had been shipped out, but they had gone on writing.
40 For thirteen months, she had faithfully replied, and more than replied.
When his letters did not arrive, she wrote anyway, and now he believed
he loved her, and she loved him.

But she had refused all his pleas to send him her photograph. That
seemed rather bad, of course. But she had explained: "If your feeling for
45 me has any reality, any honest basis, what I look like won't matter. Suppose
I'm beautiful. I'd always be haunted by the feeling that you had been taking
a chance on just that, and that kind of love would disgust me. Suppose I'm
plain (and you must admit that this is more likely) then I'd always fear that
you were going on writing to me only because you were lonely and had no
50 one else. No, don't ask for my picture. When you come to New York, you
shall see me and then you shall make your decision. Remember, both of
us are free to stop or to go on after that—whichever we choose. . . ."

One minute to six . . . he pulled hard on a cigarette.

Then Lieutenant Blandford's heart leaped higher than his plane had
55 ever done.

A young woman was coming toward him. Her figure was long and slim;
her blond hair lay back in curls from her delicate ears. Her eyes were blue
as flowers, her lips and chin had a gentle firmness. In her pale green suit,
she was like springtime come alive.
60 He started toward her, entirely forgetting to notice that she was wearing no rose, and as he moved, a small, provocative smile curved her lips.

"Going my way, soldier?" she murmured.

Uncontrollably, he made one step closer to her. Then he saw Hollis Meynell.

She was standing almost directly behind the girl, a woman well past 65 forty, her graying hair tucked under a worn hat. She was more than plump; her thick-ankled feet were thrust into low-heeled shoes. But she wore a red rose in the rumpled lapel of her brown coat.

The girl in the green suit was walking quickly away.

Blandford felt as though he were being split in two, so keen was his 70 desire to follow the girl, yet so deep was his longing for the woman whose spirit had truly companioned and upheld his own; and there she stood. Her pale, plump face was gentle and sensible; he could see that now. Her gray eyes had a warm, kindly twinkle.

Lieutenant Blandford did not hesitate. His fingers gripped the small, 75 worn, blue leather copy of *Of Human Bondage* which was to identify him to her. This would not be love, but it would be something precious, something perhaps even rarer than love—a friendship for which he had been and must ever be grateful. . . .

He squared his broad shoulders, saluted and held the book out toward 80 the woman, although even while he spoke he felt choked by the bitterness of his disappointment.

"I'm Lieutenant John Blandford, and you—you are Miss Meynell. I'm so glad you could meet me. May—may I take you to dinner?"

The woman's face broadened in a tolerant smile. "I don't know what 85 this is all about, son," she answered. "That young lady in the green suit— the one who just went by—begged me to wear this rose on my coat. And she said that if you asked me to go out with you, I should tell you that she's waiting for you in that big restaurant across the street. She said it was some kind of a test. I've got two boys with Uncle Sam myself, so I didn't mind 90 to oblige you."

The Chaser

John Collier

Alan Austen, as nervous as a kitten, went up certain dark and creaky stairs in the neighborhood of Pell Street, and peered about for a long time on the dim landing before he found the name he wanted written obscurely on one of the doors.

He pushed open this door, as he had been told to do, and found him- 5 self in a tiny room, which contained no furniture but a plain kitchen table, a rocking-chair, and an ordinary chair. On one of the dirty buff-coloured walls were a couple of shelves, containing in all perhaps a dozen bottles and jars.

10 An old man sat in the rocking-chair, reading a newspaper. Alan, without a word, handed him the card he had been given. "Sit down, Mr. Austen," said the old man very politely. "I am glad to make your acquaintance."

"Is it true," asked Alan, "that you have a certain mixture that has—er —quite extraordinary effects?"

15 "My dear sir," replied the old man, "my stock in trade is not very large—I don't deal in laxatives and teething mixtures—but such as it is, it is varied. I think nothing I sell has effects which could be precisely described as ordinary."

"Well, the fact is . . ." began Alan.

20 "Here, for example," interrupted the old man, reaching for a bottle from the shelf. "Here is a liquid as colourless as water, almost tasteless, quite imperceptible in coffee, wine, or any other beverage. It is also quite imperceptible to any known method of autopsy."

"Do you mean it is a poison?" cried Alan, very much horrified.

25 "Call it a glove-cleaner if you like," said the old man indifferently. "Maybe it will clean gloves. I have never tried. One might call it a life-cleaner. Lives need cleaning sometimes."

"I want nothing of that sort," said Alan.

"Probably it is just as well," said the old man. "Do you know the price
30 of this? For one teaspoonful, which is sufficient, I ask five thousand dollars. Never less. Not a penny less."

"I hope all your mixtures are not as expensive," said Alan apprehensively.

"Oh dear, no," said the old man. "It would be no good charging that
35 sort of price for a love potion, for example. Young people who need a love potion very seldom have five thousand dollars. Otherwise they would not need a love potion."

"I am glad to hear that," said Alan.

"I look at it like this," said the old man. "Please a customer with one
40 article, and he will come back when he needs another. Even if it *is* more costly. He will save up for it, if necessary."

"So," said Alan, "you really do sell love potions?"

"If I did not sell love potions," said the old man, reaching for another bottle, "I should not have mentioned the other matter to you. It is only
45 when one is in a position to oblige that one can afford to be so confidential."

"And these potions," said Alan. "They are not just—just—er—"

"Oh, no," said the old man. "Their effects are permanent, and extend far beyond the mere casual impulse. But they include it. Oh, yes, they include it. Bountifully, insistently. Everlastingly."

50 "Dear me!" said Alan, attempting a look of scientific detachment. "How very interesting!"

"But consider the spiritual side," said the old man.

"I do, indeed," said Alan.

"For indifference," said the old man, "they substitute devotion. For scorn, adoration. Give one tiny measure of this to the young lady—its flavour is imperceptible in orange juice, soup, or cocktails—and however gay and giddy she is, she will change altogether. She will want nothing but solitude and you."

"I can hardly believe it," said Alan. "She is so fond of parties."

"She will not like them any more," said the old man. "She will be afraid of the pretty girls you may meet."

"She will actually be jealous?" cried Alan in a rapture. "Of me?"

"Yes, she will want to be everything to you."

"She is, already. Only she doesn't care about it."

"She will, when she has taken this. She will care intensely. You will be her sole interest in life."

"Wonderful!" cried Alan.

"She will want to know all you do," said the old man. "All that has happened to you during the day. Every word of it. She will want to know what you are thinking about, why you smile suddenly, why you are look-ing sad."

"That is love!" cried Alan.

"Yes," said the old man. "How carefully she will look after you! She will never allow you to be tired, to sit in a draught, to neglect your food. If you are an hour late, she will be terrified. She will think you are killed, or that some siren has caught you."

"I can hardly imagine Diana like that!" cried Alan, overwhelmed with joy.

"You will not have to use your imagination," said the old man. "And, by the way, since there are always sirens, if by any chance you *should*, later on, slip a little, you need not worry. She will forgive you, in the end. She will be terribly hurt, of course, but she will forgive you—in the end."

"That will not happen," said Alan fervently.

"Of course not," said the old man. "But, if it did, you need not worry. She would never divorce you. Oh, no! And, of course, she will never give you the least, the very least, grounds for—uneasiness."

"And how much," said Alan, "is this wonderful mixture?"

"It is not as dear," said the old man, "as the glove-cleaner, or life-cleaner, as I sometimes call it. No. That is five thousand dollars, never a penny less. One has to be older than you are, to indulge in that sort of thing. One has to save up for it."

"But the love potion?" said Alan.

"Oh, that," said the old man, opening the drawer in the kitchen table, and taking out a tiny, rather dirty-looking phial. "That is just a dollar."

"I can't tell you how grateful I am," said Alan, watching him fill it.

"I like to oblige," said the old man. "Then customers come back, later in life, when they are better off, and want more expensive things. Here you are. You will find it very effective."

"Thank you again," said Alan. "Good-bye."

"Au revoir," said the old man.

Again, which story do you prefer? Why? Which is the superior story? In what ways is it superior? Compare your answers with those of a colleague or classmate. Students in junior- and senior-high school can be asked to compare stories and can work on answers to questions like those asked of you.

Now let me describe what has happened when students in my undergraduate methods courses have compared the two stories and have answered the questions of preference and quality. I attest that the advocacy for the two stories is split about evenly.

To the English majors in my methods class, "Appointment with Love" seems the more literal story. It has its virtues: its plot builds a sure suspense and offers an interesting "double twist" conclusion. Characters, especially the young lieutenant, seem real enough to allow some identification. If one accepts the situation, how things will work out for the lieutenant and his female correspondent piques the reader's interest. Encompassing only a few minutes of "real" time, the story uses traditional flashback technique to build background for the climax.

The reader of "The Chaser" has to suspend his sense of literal reality if he is to make anything of the story. Is the old man a devil? A demi-god? A manipulator of frail humanity? Is there anyone so *naïve* as young Alan? Is the *reader* to believe that *Alan* believes a love potion will win him his Diana? Why doesn't the author tell us whether the love potion works? Well, the old man seems sure it will; he knows Alan will return for the "life-cleaner."

Which story you like better is an answerable question. The quality of craft that is built into the story you prefer is harder to explain. One reader will opt for the tight plot of "Appointment with Love." Another will like the subtlety of "The Chaser." Another will claim identification with the situation in "Appointment with Love" but not be engaged in Alan's eerie quest. "The Chaser" is heavy with dialogue; "Appointment with Love" is insistently narrative: that is, "more happens" in "Appointment with Love."

The two writers' uses of language will appeal variously. Is "as nervous as a kitten" (p. 32, l. 1) the cliché it seems? Check the description of Lieutenant Blandford. He's "a tall young Army lieutenant" (p. 30, l. 2). Is this stereotyping at its thinnest? How about the girl who turns out to be Hollis Meynell, she of the "long and slim" figure and "blond hair" (p. 31, l. 56)?

Which story you prefer depends upon who and what you are, depends on what you value in life and in literature. If you like knowing what happens in a story, "Appointment with Love" may be your preference. If you like speculating about what might happen, you may prefer "The Chaser."

Perhaps, by now, the question of which is the superior story is creating anxiety. After all, there must be a "right" answer. Shouldn't you, as a serious reader of fiction, prefer one or the other story for certain obvious literary reasons? Won't aspects of style, structure, verisimilitude, characterization, setting, and narrative help you work from "like" toward some higher "appreciation," from a general sense of preference to a surer sense of quality?

A good story must have a good narrative structure. Obviously, then, "Appointment with Love" is the superior narrative. But a good short story must also offer psychological reality. There is less coincidence, more psychological validity in "The Chaser"; therefore, *it* must be the superior story.

In too many classrooms, there are fast "right" answers to the issue of "quality." Students are "tasteful" or "tasteless" readers according to whether their qualitative judgments square with their teacher's. They are conditioned (or forewarned) by texts to like a particular story. If they are good boys and girls, they will try to like what the text and the teacher say they should. But they won't always be good.

Although I have strong (soon-to-be-divulged) beliefs about which story is superior, the teaching issue must be pinned down here. *The role of the teacher is to involve students in issues of taste.* In getting students involved, teachers must use such questions as *"Why* do you think that?" and *"Where* in the story do you find evidence?" and *"In what way* does that seem to you good?" These are taste-building questions.

I have been in classrooms where "The Chaser" would work and "Appointment with Love" would not. In other classes at the same grade level, the situation will be reversed. But could not either story be studied in class and taste-building questions profitably asked? Taste is a terribly complex thing. Are *you* absolutely certain whether "The Chaser" or "Appointment with Love" is superior? Could you go confidently into the texts and "prove" your judgment? A complicating thought: Is one story superior in all ways—thematically, linguistically, structurally, "morally"?

As your basic strategy for probing issues of taste and of quality, you must ask students questions getting at *particular* aspects of fiction. Although you almost surely have *feelings*—however general— about the quality of any story you will teach, it is not your responsibility to go into the classroom and pronounce them. Rather than explaining what is "good," what "bad," and why, you must help students find aspects of the text worth talking about; you must provoke them to make judgments about particular things: Do A, B, and

C tie together? What might this pattern suggest? What do you think about this possibility and that? Your role is to help students find things and notice them, to help them proceed tentatively and look for relationships; you are to help students find support for all responses that are honest or valid or possible; you are to help students become dissatisfied with the quick answer and the inept (usually subjective) speculation.

Comparing two stories is just one way to begin consideration of taste and of quality. In comparing two stories, a student is invited to go beyond likes and dislikes. In deciding whether "The Chaser" or "Appointment with Love" seemed superior, my college students were led to consider those aspects of literature they have been dealing with for years. Their first impulses were to respond on the basis of identification—what seemed to them more "agreeable." But they were willing to move, promptly, to specific literary aspects. If they mentioned style or characterization, they were asked to find evidence in support of their judgments. At a less-advanced level, young students need to develop their tastes, need more practice to develop some sense of quality. Very often, such classroom discussion will not yield a true consensus. *Nor should it.* Literature isn't neat, nor is the life it reflects and creates. No critical canon will ever be explicit enough that stories can be matched against it and emerge, say, with a score of 78 per cent.

Yet too often teachers conclude good discussions, in which experience is being gained and tastes are being formed, with a pretence (long nourished by traditions of teaching) that consensus has been achieved: "Well, now that we've discussed the structure of Appointment with Love,' I think we can safely say that . . . ." If the quicksilver components of literary quality could be "safely said," we would surely put them in a ten-page pamphlet, teach them assiduously, and let issues of taste and quality be forever subordinated to a neatly enunciated critical canon.

Since print doesn't lend itself readily to the dynamics of discussion, since a fair representation of classroom discussion would occupy far more pages than are left to me, I'll here risk stating which I believe to be the superior story. I say "risk" because it is violation of what I've been arguing. In the classroom, the discussion itself would be the critique. But the questions and opinions below *do* represent the kind of specificity I would want students to demonstrate.

For this reader, "Appointment with Love" is significantly flawed, even within the limits of the "short, short" genre. Its chief flaw seems to me stylistic—more exactly, imprecise diction. The "great round clock" that "said" (not showed) "six minutes to six"

(p. 30, l. 1) is not great enough that the young pilot (recently entrusted with expensive military aircraft) needn't "narrow" his eyes "to note the exact time" (p. 30, l. 3). He is "shocked" because he cannot control his heartbeat (p. 30, l. 5). Is one normally in control of his heartbeat? The "written words" of a woman he has never met have sustained him "unfailingly" through a hellish war. Through war, perhaps, but hardly unfailingly (we learn later) when confronted with temptation:

> A young woman was coming toward him. Her figure was long and slim; her blond hair lay back in curls from her delicate ears. . . .
> He started toward her, entirely forgetting to notice that she was wearing no rose, ...
> Uncontrollably, he made one step closer to her (p. 31, l. 56).

I can identify with Blandford's response to the deliberate provocation, but I don't think it an apt instance of unfailing sustenance at this, the moment of confrontation with the woman "he believed he loved" (p. 31, l. 41).

Blandford "placed himself as close as he could to the information booth, ..." How? *Placed* suggests to me some kind of exterior manipulation—a chess player placing a pawn, a puppeteer setting his marionette. Did Blandford walk? Sidle? Edge? How, in another case, does one's face "grow sharp" (p. 31, l. 22)? And what is the meaning of "For thirteen months, she had faithfully replied, and more than replied" (p. 31, l. 40)? How does one "more than reply"?

Too often, in this tightly structured story, language approaches but falls short of success. "Under the immense, starred roof, people were walking fast, like threads of color being woven into a gray web" (p. 31, l. 24). My recollection of Grand Central Station confirms the author's perception, but the weaving metaphor (within the simile) fails: people don't leave trails of color behind them as they walk. There is infelicitous figure: "Lieutenant Blandford's heart leaped higher than his plane had ever done" (p. 31, l. 54). Nor do I derive any physical individuality or precision in the description of the two main characters: Blandford, a "tall young Army lieutenant" with "sunburned face" (p. 30, l. 2); and she who turns out to be Hollis Meynell after all, a young woman whose

> . . . figure was long and slim; her blond hair lay back in curls from her delicate ears. Her eyes were blue as flowers, her lips and chin had a gentle firmness. In her pale green suit, she was like springtime come alive (p. 31, l. 56).

I like "springtime come alive," but in truth I don't envision "delicate ears" nor am I sure of that gently firm chin. What particular blue flower do Hollis Meynell's eyes resemble?

There are other details I hesitate over. Blandford's seeing "the grinning face of one of the enemy pilots," a serviceable visual cliché for Hollywood but not really functional here. Doesn't the reader deserve one sample of Hollis' marginal comments in *Of Human Bondage?* One example might convince me that her remarks "were different" and that she had an ability to "see into a man's heart so tenderly, so understandingly" (p. 31, l. 36). If I grant Blandford's ability to tell "a woman's writing" from a man's, I admit to his knowing that the name Hollis belongs to a woman. But *Webster's Seventh* lists Hollis under men's names, not under women's. And how does Blandford know Hollis Meynell lives in New York City? He doesn't, I think, unless that fact was on the bookplate.

There are issues that touch on the theme of the story. Blandford's behavior when confronting the three women, closely examined, gives me the feeling that he gets better than he deserves. And although things will probably go well once Blandford and Hollis Meynell get together in the restaurant, the nature of Hollis' "test" gives pause. She poses a severe (unfair?) test for a man just home from thirteen months of combat. But Blandford, after feeling "as though he were being split in two" (p. 32, l. 70), does the decent thing. What has he won? A beautiful woman who wants to be loved for more than her beauty, a woman who if she did not provide this test, would "always be haunted by the feeling" (p. 31, l. 46) that Blandford is on the prowl for someone who is physically attractive." . . . [T]hat kind of love would disgust me" (p. 31, l. 47). Indeed, the Lieutenant and Hollis Meynell will have a lot to talk about.

The outstanding quality of "Appointment with Love" is its plot, and managing so successful a plan is no mean feat. The chief failure of the story is in its language, especially in its imprecise diction.[11]

11. In negotiating for permission to reprint "Appointment with Love," I encountered an animated and friendly spirit in Miss S. I. Kishor, author of "Appointment with Love," among much other published work. Miss Kishor was understandably reluctant to grant permission for use of her story without seeing the context for its use. Several letters, several phone calls, and one lively meeting later, Miss Kishor granted me permission to use her story. She requested that I change some of the comments I'd written. In truth, the changes she suggested improved both the focus and the quality of my critique. Miss Kishor provided a rebuttal to my comments. It is a privilege to print here, with her approval, that rebuttal:

Those who like "Appointment with Love" better than "The Chaser" are perhaps realizing that a "short, short story" is, by definition, very brief, yet it can tell a great deal. Its effects must be gained as quickly as possible. Such expressions as "his face grew sharp" are, therefore, a kind of literary shorthand, to indicate in four words what might otherwise require fourteen.

You may also see that in this story, as in most short shorts, there is a background, implied rather than expressed. It is made clear that Hollis Meynell is a very beautiful girl who is also

Is not "The Chaser" the better story? There are things to think about, if one wants to think. On a symbolic level the question of what happens when man turns to magic potions to get what he wants out of life suggests something of the fate of people looking for easy answers to knotty problems. The old man is a stock character—and the author avoids giving him any characterization (or even a name) that will allow the reader to miss the stereotype. Alan is a stock character, too: color him naïve. The basic subtlety of the story is that the plot line must be resolved by the reader. The climax of the story occurs three or four paragraphs *after* the print ends. Will Alan administer the love potion? Will Diana become the possessive, adoring female Alan thinks he wants her to become? Will Alan subsequently go back for the "life-cleaner"?

Answers are clearly implied. *"Au revoir,"* says the old man after Alan says "Good-bye." Alan believes he *is* saying good-bye; but the old man knows perfectly well what "au revoir" means.

There are subtleties—the irony, for example, of the old man's "She would never divorce you" (p. 34, l. 85). At first glance this seems the way things *should* be; on second look it's clear that Alan will have to do away with his potion-charged ladylove in order to escape her obsessive attentions. Diana is probably named with some care: Does she echo the goddess of the moon? Of the hunt? Who is the hunted, and who the hunter?

The title of the story works on several levels. A chaser is, first, a drink like water that follows a shot of liquor. An extension of meaning ties the love potion and its chaser with a glass of liquor

intelligent and serious-minded. All her life, men have been after her because of her looks; no one notices her as a human being. So she is delighted when this apparently fine young man is attracted by her intelligence and understanding.

But—has he perhaps seen her picture in local society columns, where it has often appeared? Does he perhaps *know* she is a beauty and of well-to-do family? Could all this be a trick? She plans this device to find out: (1) will he recognize her as she passes by, without the rose; and (2) if he does not know her, but believes this middle-aged, "frowsy" woman is the one who has been writing him, how will he solve his problem? Will he hurt, humiliate, and disappoint the woman by escaping from the scene, or will he find some way to let her down easily?

Which kind of man is Blandford? If the first kind, he is no different from any other man she has met. If the second, he is a man whom she can respect and trust, and marry.

The question of the story is not merely "What does this girl look like?" but also, "What kind of character has the soldier?"

Hollis' character is indicated not only in the implied background, which the reader unconsciously absorbs; it is completed by the final sentence of the story. Hollis has carefully selected her "stand-in": a plain, middle-aged woman but not a repulsive one; not a sad, lonely one who might have false hopes aroused by the handsome lieutenant's invitation, but a woman who is a contented wife and mother.

Those who like the more sophisticated, ironic quality of "The Chaser" are appreciating its impeccable wit and fantasy as well as its biting comment on human nature; those who prefer "Appointment with Love" are putting the emphasis on an emotionally satisfying story. They may be showing dislike of the hatred and scorn of humanity implied in "The Chaser" and confirming their own optimism and faith as expressed in "Appointment with Love."

S. I. Kishor

and its chaser. A chaser is, on another level, one who chases, first an Alan, then a Diana.

Stylistically, "The Chaser" is clean and efficient. Even cliché is used to good purpose. Alan, "as nervous as a kitten," is also as innocent as a kitten, as we discover. The setting is sure, the old man's bottles and jars standing out sharply in his sparsely furnished room. Alan reveals himself through the lines he speaks and the questions he asks. The (prototypical) character of Diana can be pretty well inferred even though she never actually appears in the story. The author of "The Chaser" provides an entertainment, offers in that entertainment some interesting questions about life (what it's like or might be like); he performs an imaginative act that seems to me superior to the device of a surprise ending.

As with the discussion of "Appointment with Love," I would try to hold off my own judgments, but I would surely reflect them in getting students to deal with particulars. If the setting of "The Chaser" were to be discussed, I might ask "teaching" questions about the story's geography (Why " . . . in the neighborhood of Pell Street"?) and about the diction ("certain dark and creaky stairs," "the dim landing," and the "obscurely" written name). Answers to such questions, which are more or less factual, may come from me (the Pell Street neighborhood in New York City hints at exotic merchandise and shady transactions) or from students (who can add up the effect of darkness and dimness and obscurity). But in either case the idea is to develop and interpret information that is rooted in text.

Pell Street and Collier's diction are there to be looked at. Yet the "learning" questions are often more important. Here the answers are less certain. Are there ties among the setting, the character of "the old man," and his peculiar merchandise? A variety of answers may emerge, some more reasonable than others. Some may extend interpretation; others will narrow it. But there is no single "right" answer. Uncertainty will often (and properly) return us to the text: what clues have been overlooked?

Although I find "The Chaser" the superior story, I've been in classes where "Appointment with Love" would be the better-liked story and an appropriate story to build taste from. With either story, an investigation of taste and of the quality of the performance can be undertaken. The technique of comparing particular aspects of stories will promote a sense of what quality in fiction is. The necessity is that students must become involved in the questions of taste.

If taste *is* an issue, we must give students practice in developing it. As soon as a primitive judgment is made, that judgment should first be tested against the available data on which judgment is based:

in the case of fiction, judgment begins with the print on the page. The performance of the writer can be talked about qualitatively, and this is what literary criticism seeks to do. In class-room terms this means looking at such aspects as theme, structure, use of language, dialect, and characterization. With other stories, it means attention to point-of-view and to rhetoric. It means ultimately the making of a judgment on how well these aspects are brought together in the total performance.

So far we have talked of teaching advantages inherent in the short story form and have considered four teaching principles for short stories: (1) limiting the aims in the teaching of any story; (2) focusing upon the text of the story; (3) moving from concrete to abstract in extending our considerations; and (4) approaching taste in fiction as an issue. In the two sections following, we hear from two well-known (and very dissimilar) writers of short stories, Jack Schaefer and Roald Dahl. They talk about teaching literature, in general, and then talk particularly about teaching stories of their own. Both writers wonder whether literature can be taught at all; both then proceed to "teach" stories of their own.

BIOGRAPHICAL NOTE

Photo: Andy Gregg

Born in Cleveland, Ohio, in 1907, Jack Schaefer graduated from Oberlin College in 1929, worked for the United Press, for the Connecticut State Reformatory, and as an editor and writer for a variety of newspapers. In 1949, his *Shane* was published by Houghton Mifflin. Its runaway success permitted Schaefer to devote himself to writing. (*Shane* has a mystique all its own: one United States senator claims to be the only human alive to have seen the film first in Seattle and then in Fairbanks, Alaska, on consecutive nights. A high school senior I know has made a school career of reading and reporting on *Shane*—reporting on it each year since seventh grade.)

Jack Schaefer's stories and books deal with the Western frontier. His themes and settings are authentic. His skill at characterization has brought critical praise from serious students of literature and has placed him in the company of Oliver LaFarge, Conrad Richter, and Stephen Crane. Students in the schools know him through such stories as "Harvey Kendall," "The Old Man," and "Jacob" (which begins on page 51).

Schaefer and his wife, Louise, live in Santa Fe in a three-hundred-year-old Spanish hacienda "of at least seventeen rooms." It is "inconvenient as hell," Schaefer writes, "but it has its own voice, and it speaks to me gently and clearly: 'So you finally got here, where you belong.'"

His more than a dozen books include:

Shane	Houghton Mifflin,	1949
The Canyon	Houghton Mifflin,	1953
The Pioneers	Houghton Mifflin,	1954
Company of Cowards	Houghton Mifflin,	1957
Old Ramon	Houghton Mifflin,	1960
Monte Walsh	Houghton Mifflin,	1963
Heroes Without Glory	Houghton Mifflin,	1965

Two recent collections, *The Collected Stories of Jack Schaefer* and *The Collected Short Novels of Jack Schaefer,* both published by Houghton Mifflin, provide a comprehensive introduction to this cactus-crossed teller of tales. The essay and stories following show him as I know him—lively, opinionated, and wise.

PART TWO

If Stories Must Be Taught

Jack Schaefer

I assert as simple truth that literature cannot be taught. Certainly not at the below-college level.

The history of literature can be taught—names and titles and dates and labels for literary movements. But the attempt to teach literature itself degenerates into a form of petty torture inflicted on captive students and succeeds chiefly in convincing most of them that the written word when tainted with academic approval is something to be avoided for the rest of their lives. The few who survive with actual fondness for the stuff are susceptible in advance. They catch the contagion, like measles, from mere exposure. The rest are immunized effectively and forever.

Literature cannot be taught. Should not be taught. The teaching takes on the character of a crime. A work of literature can be as tough as whipcord in the writing, strong and sinewy and well-knit; but the ultimate ingredient which gives it life, which makes it literature, is an elusive essence of spirit that can not be abstracted, isolated, identified. When a poem, a short story, a novel has been analyzed, dissected, it becomes a dead thing with the life gone. Discussion of it is a wake held over a corpse. It has been killed by the well-intentioned but deadly application of the belief (sanctified by the successes of modern science in other fields) that the way to grasp the essentials of a subject is to break it down into its component parts, to describe it in physical equations or chemical formulae, to reduce it to a compilation of technical terms. You might as well say that the morning breeze sweeping out of the Mountains of Imagination is a mixture in motion of oxygen and nitrogen in about the proportions of one to four with traces of argon and neon and other rare gases. It is not. It is the morning breeze.

The teacher who steps out in front of a batch of stubborn young minds encased in the callow carcasses of boys and girls and cherishes high-flying idealistic notions of teaching them literature is a misguided misguiding fool. The attitude is wrong; the approach; even the purpose. Youngsters cannot run before they have learned to walk, fly before they have sprouted mental wings. The one and only one decent justifiable purpose for any so-called class in literature is not to try to teach literature, but to try to teach a neglected almost forgotten skill—reading. Not to teach specific poems or short stories or novels. These are but means to an end. Simply to teach the ability to read, if possible the habit of reading, with some measure of discernment and understanding—perhaps even some measure of enjoyment.

Oh, by this time the youngsters (most of them) know how to read in the literal sense of the word. They know that c-a-t spells cat and some may have advanced to add other letters into c-a-tegory. But only a rare few come from homes in which books are present— not just as wall or table top decorations—or have parents with the inclination and will power occasionally to turn off the television and pick up and even open one of those peculiar objects with bindings outside and pages inside. Only a few have even begun to make a start at learning how really to read. The rest are illiterate in a literary sense—do not know how to read for anything more than the mere bald generalized gist of the words. And to them even that kind of nonreading is to be done only in default of anything else or under the whip of necessity—waiting in a doctor's or a dentist's office or meeting the minimum of a class assignment.

This is not the youngsters' fault. They have been growing up in a barbaric suspicious-of-culture everything-must-have-practical-application society which seems determined to keep young minds swaddled in half pure-white and half violent-hued cotton batting. On the one hand, asinine children's books written down to cater to little minds, not written up to stretch growing minds, school reading texts full of pallid pap, and simplified expurgated condensed life-squeezed-out versions of classics. On the other hand, gory comic books that massacre the mother tongue, ubiquitous advertisements and commercial slogans that defy grammar and precise meaning, and television programs deliberately throttled down to the lowest common denominator of mass moronicism. Of course youngsters are illiterate. They have been rather successfully insulated against any but the most cursory contact with the strengths and the subtleties of the very language they think they speak.

Picture-books, picture-magazines, expurgation, sterilization, simplification, condensation—now speed-reading as something to be admired and sought. The illusion is that to have skimmed rapidly through a book and caught the main points if it is nonfiction and the plot-outline if it is a story is to have read that book. Everywhere the decline of and disrespect for the printed word except as a means of propaganda or of conveying quick brittle bare-boned information. Hurrah! I can read *Hamlet* in twenty minutes and tell you who killed whom and how many corpses were heaped at the finish! It's *almost* as good as a gangster comic book!

To try to teach literature at the below-college level (and often above) is of necessity to teach reading.

I take for granted that the teacher knows how to read. Out of deference to the feminine majority among teachers I use the feminine pronouns. She knows how to read—knows that true reading is more than a passive reception of printed symbols on a page, is an active exercise of the mind and the emotions. She knows how to read or she has no right to teach, regardless of degrees and certificates and other official nonsense. She should demonstrate that exotic unpopular ability she has somehow acquired. She is a fake, a swindler not earning even her relatively low salary, if she simply assigns outside reading for her students and then gabbles about it in class. She should do considerable of their reading for them. She should read aloud to them often and often.

Literature is a maimed art, crippled by being printed in books. It began as a vocal art and would still be at its best as a vocal art—the writer "speaking" directly to his audience. It is printed in books for preservation and for multiplication of "listeners" not only in contemporary numbers but on through time into later generations. But in being put into books, literature loses much. In the cold flat orderly progression of words on pages there are no variations of tone, of emphasis, of emotional stress; no changes of pace, no pregnant pauses, no quickenings and risings towards climaxes, no nuances of sound and the responses these can evoke. There are only ink marks on a once-virgin whiteness.

The writer has tried, with the words he has used, with the way he has used them, the calculated progression of them, with their arrangement on the page, with the limited typographical tricks available to him, with the aid of the few expressive punctuation marks custom and grammarians permit, to suggest what his voice would be doing were he speaking directly. He has tried to indicate how he wants his words to reach the mind's ear of the "listener." He has done his best to imbed the "sounds" in the print. And there, alas, for all he can do about it, they remain—unless and until a reader, a "listener," makes the mental effort to summon them forth.

The supposed reader who skims for the story, who passively lets the images of the printed words slide across the retinas of his eyes with nothing more than the silent generalized meaning penetrating to his brain, never "hears" those "sounds" the writer has put into the print. He misses not only them but the overtones they conjure into being, the pulse of life they give to the whole, the subtle extra significance which has made it literature. He sees the words. He may even out-guess the teacher on which silly details she may base questions as a check on the supposed reading. But he does not read—not as literature must be read. He merely goes through the outward motions. He fails to comprehend the difference between literature and routine writing because he cannot "hear" the "sounds" that are the signs of the life in the one that is lacking in the other. He can detect no difference—except that what the teacher insists on calling literature is more difficult to get through, harder to grasp even in the generalized gist, and therefore very likely more a waste of time. He is apt to conclude that the teacher is talking high-faluting nonsense that is worth enduring solely for course credit.

It is the task of the teacher to try to show that there *is* a difference, a rewarding difference, that the "sounds" are there, imprisoned in the print, waiting to be released. It is her job to be the "voice" of the writer. And perhaps, by constant example, to convince her students that the true reader can learn to summon that "voice" at will from the printed page.

Literature cannot be taught. But how to read with reasonable skill can be—within the limits of natural capabilities. Some will never learn it. But others will. And to those who really learn to read, literature teaches itself. If the teacher shrewdly chooses stories with "voices" students may think worth listening to, literature can lead them on to the desire to "hear" more "voices"—to increasing ability to "listen" to ever more subtle and stronger and wiser "voices."

Let the teacher teach her students to break through the barrier of print, to recognize in printed words the voice of another human being speaking to them, reciting a poem to convey a sincere emotion or insight, telling a tale because it has significance for him, making a comment in a novel on the world in which he lives, and literature will do very well on its own. That is its reason for being—to speak, to communicate.

The big things can wait. To spend a semester plowing grimly through a few long works is sheer absurdity. It is to succumb to the ridiculous notion that the purpose is to teach specific items of literature—when the one valid purpose is to teach the ability (and the willingness) to read any and many items of literature, to encourage a friendly attitude towards all literature. No literature course can ever be more than a sampling process. A long series of courses could do no more than to cover a few tiny fractions of a few small segments of a few selected areas of the vast field of the world's literature. To confine the sampling to a few long works is to cheat the students. Of what value is it to have pounded into their heads an isolated soon-forgotten acquaintance with an *Ivanhoe* or a *Julius Caesar* or a *Silas Marner*, unless a desire to read more literature, perhaps and hopefully a lifetime habit of reading it, has been developed in at least some of them? Short things are best for this. The more that can be adequately covered, the better.

Not excerpts, selections from, dismemberments! Such are like chunks of dead meat in a butcher's shop! The complete animal each time or none of it at all!

A work of literature is a living organism, conceived as a whole, created as a whole. However much he labored on separate parts, the writer visioned it whole, strove to make it whole. To pick it to pieces, to take it apart in the process of reading, is an insult to him. He has given it individuality. It has its own style, its own tone, its own internal rhythms, its own over-all shape. The effect the writer sought comes from the totality of it. Appreciation of it, discussion of it, is meaningless unless launched from that perspective—from the thing seen and "heard" and felt complete, alive and functioning. The more individual items a student can grasp in this way, the more he may begin to realize the endless wondrous variety and the tremendous scope of the land of literature waiting for any willing explorer.

What the writer has achieved is far more important than *how* he achieved it. The what, the essential whatness, the cumulative final effect, is the goal he sought—and should be the goal sought by the reader. Only when that has been reached does study of the how make sense. And then only insofar as it can deepen appreciation of the what. Too much talk about techniques can be a trap, can all too easily become an end in itself.

Of what worth is it to a student to be able to identify the point-of-view a writer uses in telling a tale—unless he can grasp why the writer chose that particular point-of-view to add to the full effect of that particular tale? Of what worth to be able to spot methods of characterization—unless he can understand the character characterized and what the writer felt and thought and meant to communicate with and about that character? Of what worth to be able to point out elements of style—unless he can relate these to the work as a whole and recognize which are peculiar to this particular work and aid in producing its vital result? Of what worth to be able to pick out examples of foreshadowing of later events in a story—unless he can see how these are fitted into the over-all form of that story to heighten tension and anticipation of the climax they foreshadow? Of what worth to be able to find and label correctly the various figures of speech spotted through a narrative—unless he can relate these to the work as a whole and realize what they contribute in setting the tone, adding to the atmosphere, underlining the meaning? Of what worth to be able to sort out symbols—unless he can comprehend what the writer has done with them, what significance and emphasis they impart to the finished work?

Techniques are nothing in themselves. They take on value only as they contribute to the totality of the whole—which, if it is literature, has become something above and beyond them. A writer can be expert in using them—and still fail in the writing. His very expertness can get in his way. If he is too conscious of techniques, too deliberate and calculating in his use of them, he ends up manufacturing, not writing, a manuscript. He has concocted a mixture of gases in what scientific research has told him are the right proportions. It remains a mixture. It is not the morning breeze.

In the same way a reader can be expert in recognizing techniques, can be glib in prattle of technical terms—and still fail in the reading. In the old saying, he cannot see the forest for the trees. Too much attention to the separate components has obscured the whole—which is the sole reason for there being any components. Another reader, blissfully ignorant of technical jargon but interested in what the writer has done, not how he has done it, may "hear" much more of what the writer sought to communicate.

Short things, many of them, that can be grasped as living wholes, as separate works of art conceived and wrought and shaped by fellow human beings striving to break through the barrier of print and speak to their fellows. Not cold print on pages, but resonant human voices caught there and waiting for the welcome of release. In each case not something dead and buried in ink and preserved as a kind of antique curiosity in a museum, but something alive in the always immediate present and merely sleeping there and waiting to be awakened.

Short things, many of them read aloud and savored in the reading. Not read punctuated by interruptions—aha, here the writer is doing this, here he is doing that, and aren't we smart to catch him at his technical tricks and know the names for them. No! Each read straight through for the flavor and continuity of the writing, for the feeling of the whole, for the sense of it as a living entity. Then discussion of what the writer has been doing, what he has been trying his best to do and to say. And one of the fascinating aspects of true literature is that the same poem or story or novel can say different things to different readers. The differences are not so much in what actually is said as in the shades of meaning seen in it, for inevitably all readers must interpret it in terms of their own individual experiences, knowledges, thoughts, emotions, even prejudices.

The entity, the organism, that was imprisoned in the print has been released, seen and "heard" as something complete and finished and moving to its full final effect. Then, perhaps, a brief review of it to point out for the more amateur readers aspects they have missed or whose significance to the whole they have overlooked. And then, then only, and with restraint, discussion of *how* the writer achieved his *what.*

But always, insofar as possible, all discussion in terms of the work as a work of art, complete in itself, conceived and shaped to that completeness. Not as a mixture of gases in motion—but as a message borne on the morning breeze!

Jacob

Jack Schaefer

Those moccasins? Mine. Though I never wore them. Had them on just once to see if they fitted. They did. A bit tight but I could get them on.

Don't touch them. The leather's old and dry and the stitching rotted. Ought to be. They've been hanging there a long time. Look close and you can see the craftsmanship. The best. They're Nez Percé moccasins. Notice the design worked into the leather. It's faint now but you can make it out. Don't know how they did that but the Nez Percé could really work leather. A professor who studied such things told me once that design means they're for a chief. For his ceremonial appearances, sort of his dress-up footwear. Said only a chief could use that design. But it's there. Right there on those moccasins.

Yes. They're small. Boy size. That's because I was a boy then. But they're a chief's moccasins all the same. Kept them down the years because I'm proud of them. And because they mind me of a man. He had a red skin.

Copper would be closer the color. A muddy copper. And I only saw him once. But he was a man.

That was a long way from here. A long way. In years and in miles. I was ten then, maybe eleven, maybe twelve, in that neighborhood, I disremember exactly. Best I can do is place it in the late seventies. Funny how definite things like dates and places slip away and other stray things, like the way you felt at certain times and how your first wild strawberries tasted, can remain clear and sharp in your mind. We were living, my folks and my older brother and myself, in a little town in eastern Montana. Not much of a place. Just a small settlement on the railroad that wouldn't have amounted to anything except that it had a stretch of double track where a train going one direction could pull off to let one going the other get past. My father was a switchman. Looked after track and handled the west-end switch. That was why we were there.

The Indian smell was still in the air in those days. People around here and nowadays wouldn't know what that means. It was a knowing and a remembering that not so far away were still real live free-footed fighting Indians that might take to raiding again. They were pegged on treaty lands and supposed to stay there. But they were always hot over one thing or another, settlers gnawing into their hunting grounds or agents pinching their rations or maybe the government forgetting to keep up treaty payments. You never knew when they might get to figuring they'd been pushed far enough and would start council fires up in the hills and come sudden and silent out of the back trails, making trouble. It was only a year or two since the Custer affair on the Little Big Horn southwest of where we were. No-one with any experience in those things expected the treaty that ended that business to hold long.

Don't take me wrong. We didn't look for Indians behind bushes and sit around shivering at night worrying about attacks. The nearest reservation was a fair jump away and if trouble started we'd know about it long before it reached us, if it ever did. Matter of fact it never did. I grew up in that territory and never once was mixed in any Indian trouble past an argument over the price of a blanket. Never even saw any fighting Indians except this once I'm telling about and then they weren't fighting any more. It was just a smell in the air, the notion there might be trouble any time. Indians were quite a topic when I was a boy and the talk of an evening chewed it plenty.

Expect I heard as much of it as any of the boys around our settlement. Maybe more. My father had been in the midst of the Sioux outbreak in Minnesota in the early sixties. He'd seen things that would harden a man. They settled his mind on the subject. "Only good Indian," he'd say, "is a dead one." Yes. That's not just a saying out of the storybooks. There were men who really said it. And believed it. My father was one. Said it and believed it and said it so often I'd not be stretching the truth past shape to figure he averaged it couple times a week and so naturally we boys believed it too, hearing it all the time. I'll not argue with anyone wants to believe it even today. I'm only telling you what happened to me.

Hearing that kind of talk we boys around the settlement had our idea what Indians were like. I can speak for myself anyway. The Indians I saw sometimes passing through on a train or loafing around a town the few times I was in one with the folks didn't count. They were tame ones. They were scrawny mostly and they hung around where white people were and traded some and begged liquor when they couldn't buy it. They weren't dangerous or even interesting. They didn't matter more'n mules or dogs or anything like that cluttering the landscape. It was the wild ones filled my mind, the fighting kind that lived the way they always had and went on the warpath, and made the government send out troops and sign treaties with them. Can't recall exactly what I thought they looked like, but they were big and fierce and dangerous and they liked to burn out homesteaders' cabins and tie people to wagon wheels and roast them alive over slow fires, and it took a brave man to go hunting them and look at them down the sights of his gun. Days I felt full of ginger I'd plan to grow up quick and be an Indian fighter. Late afternoon, before evening chores, I'd scout the countryside with the stick I used for a gun and when I'd spot a spray of red sumac poking out of a brush clump, I'd belly-it in the grass and creep to good cover and poke my gun through and draw my bead. I'd pull on the twig knob that was my trigger and watch careful, and sometimes I'd have to fire again and then I'd sit up and cut another notch on the stick. I had my private name for that. Making good Indians, I called it.

What's that got to do with those moccasins? Not much I guess. But I'm telling this my way. It's all part of what I remember when I sit back and study those moccasins a spell.

The year I'm talking about was a quiet one with the Sioux but there was some Indian trouble all right, along in the fall and a ways away, over in the Nez Percé country in Idaho. It started simple enough like those things often did. There was this band lived in a valley, maybe seven hundred of them all told, counting the squaws and young ones. Biggest safe estimate I heard was three hundred braves, fighting men I mean. Can't remember the name of the valley, though I should. My brother settled there. But I can recall the name of the chief. That sticks. Always will. Not the Indian of it because that was a fancy mouthful. What it meant. Mountain Elk. Not that exactly. Big-Deer-That-Walks-the-High-Places. Mountain Elk is close enough. But people didn't call him that. Most Indians had a short name got tagged to them somehow and were called by it. His was Jacob. Sounded funny first time I heard it but not after I'd been hearing it a while.

As I say, this trouble started simple enough. We heard about it from the telegraph operator at the settlement who took his meals at our place. He picked up information relaying stuff through his key. News of all kinds and even military reports. Seems settlers began closing in around Jacob's valley and right soon began looking at the land there. Had water which was important in that country. Some of them pushed in and Jacob and his boys pushed them back out. So complaints were being made and more people wanted to move in, and talk went around that land like that was too good for Indians anyway because they didn't use it right, the way white men would, and when there was enough steam up a government man went in to see Jacob. Suggested the band would be better off living on some outside reservation. Get regular rations and have an agent to look after them. No, Jacob said, he and his were doing all right. Had been for quite a spell and expected to keep on doing the same. Sent his thanks to the Great White Chief for thinking about him but he wasn't needing any help. So after a while the pressure was stronger and another government man went in. Offered to buy the land and move the band in style to a reservation. No, said Jacob, he and his children—he called them all his children though he wasn't much past thirty himself—he and his children liked their land and weren't interested in selling. Their fathers had given up land too much in the past and been forced to keep wandering and had found this place when no one wanted it, and it was good and they had stayed there. Most of them then living had been born there and they wanted to die there too and that was that.

Well, the pressure went on building and there were ruckuses here and yonder around the valley when some more settlers tried moving in and a bunch of young braves got out of hand and killed a few. So another government man went in, this time with a soldier escort. He didn't bother with arguing or bargaining. He told Jacob the Great White Chief had issued a decree and this was that the whole tribe was to be moved by such and such a date. If they went peaceable, transportation would be provided and good rations. If they kept on being stubborn, soldiers would come and make them move and that would be a bad business all around. Yes, said Jacob, that would be a bad business but it wouldn't be his doing. He and his children wouldn't have made the storm but they would stand up to it if it came. He had spoken and that was that.

So the days went along toward the date set which was in the fall I'm telling about. Jacob and his band hadn't made any preparations for leaving and the officer in charge of this whole operation thought Jacob was bluffing and he'd just call that bluff. He sent about four hundred soldiers under some colonel into the valley the week before the moving was supposed to happen, and Jacob and the others, the whole lot of them, just faded away from their village and off into the mountains behind the valley. The colonel sent scouting parties after them but couldn't make contact. He didn't know what to do in that situation so he set up camp there in the valley to wait and got real peeved when some of Jacob's Nez Percés slipped down out of the mountains one night and stampeded his stock. Finally he had his new orders and on the supposed moving day he carried them out. He put his men to destroying the village and they wiped it level to the ground, and the next morning early there was sharp fighting along his upper picket lines and he lost quite a few men before he could jump his troops into the field in decent force.

That was the beginning. The government wanted to open the valley for homesteading but couldn't without taking care of Jacob first. This colonel tried. He chased Jacob and his band into the mountains and thought overtaking them would be easy with the squaws and young ones slowing Jacob down, but Jacob had hidden them off somewhere and was traveling light with his braves. He led this colonel a fast run through rough country and caught him off watch a few times and whittled away at his troops every odd chance till this colonel had to turn back, not being outfitted for a real campaign. When he, that'd be this colonel, got back he found Jacob had beat him there and made things mighty unpleasant for those left holding the camp before slipping away again. About this time the government realized what it was up against and recalled the colonel and maybe whoever was his boss, and assigned a general—a brigadier—to the job and began mounting a real expedition.

We heard plenty about what happened after that, not just from the telegraph operator but from my brother who was busting the seams of his breeches those days and wanting to strike out for himself, and signed with the freighting company that got the contract carting supplies for the troops. He didn't see any of the fighting but he was close to it several times and he wrote home what was happening. Once a week he'd promised to write and did pretty well at it. He'd send his letters along to be posted whenever any of the wagons were heading back, and my mother would read them out to my father and me when they arrived. Remember best the fat one came after he reached the first camp and saw Jacob's valley. Took him two chunks of paper both sides to tell about it. Couldn't say enough about the thick green grass and the stream tumbling into a small lake and running quiet out again, and the good trees stepping up the far slopes and the mountains climbing on to the end of time all around. Made a man want to put his feet down firm on the ground and look out steady like the standing trees and stretch tall. Expect that's why my brother quit his job soon as the trouble was over and drove his own stakes there.

Yes. I know. I'm still a long way from those moccasins. I'm over in Idaho in Jacob's valley. But I get to remembering and then I get to forgetting maybe you're not interested in all the sidelines of what I started to tell you. I'll try to move it faster.

As I was saying, the government outfitted a real expedition to go after Jacob. A brigadier general and something like a thousand men. There's no point telling all that happened except that this expedition didn't accomplish much more than that first colonel and his men did. They chased Jacob farther and almost penned him a few times and killed a lot of braves and got wind of where his women and their kids were hidden, and forced him to move them farther into the mountains with them getting out just in time, not being able to carry much with them. But that wasn't catching Jacob and stopping him and his braves from carrying on their hop-skip-and-jump war against all whites in general and these troops in particular. Then a second general went in and about a thousand more soldiers with them and they had hard fighting off and on over a couple hundred miles and more, and the days drove on into deep winter and Jacob was licked. Not by the government and its soldiers and their guns. By the winter. He and his braves, what was left of them, had kept two generals and up to two thousand troops busy for four months fighting through parts of three states and then the winter licked him. He came to the second general under truce in what remained of his Chief's rig and took off his headdress and laid it on the ground and spoke. His children were scattered in the mountains, he said, and the cold bit sharp and they had few blankets and no food. Several of the small ones had been found frozen to death. From the moment the sun passed overhead that day he would fight no more. If he was given time to search for his children and bring them together he would lead them wherever the Great White Chief wished.

There. I'm closer to those moccasins now even though I'm still way over in Idaho. No. Think it was in western Montana where Jacob surrendered to that second general. Well, the government decided to ship these Nez Percés to the Dump, which was what people called the Indian Territory where they chucked all the tribes whose lands weren't just cut down but were taken away altogether. That meant Jacob and his children, all that was left of them, about three hundred counting the squaws and kids, would be loaded on a special train and sent along the railroad that ran through our settlement. These Nez Percé Indians would be passing within a stone's throw of our house and we would have a chance to see them at least through the windows and maybe, if there was need for switching, the train would stop and we would have a good look.

Wonder if you can scratch up any real notion what that meant to us boys around the settlement. To me maybe most of all. These weren't tame Indians. These were wild ones. Fighting Indians. About the fightingest Indians on record. Sure, the Sioux wiped out Custer. But there were a lot more Sioux than soldiers in that scuffle. These Nez Percés had held their own mighty well against a big chunk of the whole United States Army of those days. They were so outnumbered it had got past being even a joke. Any way you figured, it had been about one brave to six or seven soldiers and those braves hadn't been well armed at the start and had to pick up guns and ammunition as they went along from soldiers they killed. Some of them were still using arrows at the finish. I'm not being funny when I tell you they kept getting bigger and fiercer in my mind all the time I was hearing about that long running fight in the mountains. It was notches for Nez Percés I was cutting on my stick now and the way I felt about them, even doing that took nerve.

The day came the train was to pass through, some time late afternoon was the first report, and all of us settlement boys stayed near the telegraph shack waiting. It was cold, though there wasn't much snow around. We'd sneak into the shack where there was a stove, till the operator was peeved at our chattering and shooed us out, and I expect I did more than my share of the chattering because in a way these were my Indians because my brother was connected with the expedition that caught them. Don't think the other boys liked how I strutted about that. Well, anyway, the sun went down and we all had to scatter home for supper and the train hadn't come. Afterwards some of us slipped back to the shack and waited some more while the operator cussed at having to stick around waiting for word, and one by one we were yanked away when our fathers came looking for us, and still the train hadn't come.

It was some time past midnight and I'd finally got to sleep when I popped up in bed at a hammering on the door. I looked into the kitchen. Father was there in his nightshirt opening the outside door and the operator was on the step cussing some more that he'd had word the train was coming, would get there in half an hour, and they'd have to switch it and hold it till the westbound night freight went past. Father added his own cussing and pulled on his pants and boots and heavy jacket and lit his lantern. By time he'd done that I had my things on too. My mother was up then and objecting, but my father thought some and shushed her. "Fool kid," he said, "excited about Indians all the time. Do him good to see what thieving smelly things they are." So I went with him. The late moon was up and we could see our way easy and I stayed in the shack with the operator and my father went off to set his signal and tend his switch. Certain enough, in about twenty minutes the train came along and swung onto the second line of track and stopped.

The telegraph operator stepped out and started talking to a brakeman. I was scared stiff. I stood in the shack doorway and looked at the train and I was shaking inside like I had some kind of fever. It wasn't much of a train. Just an engine and little fuel car and four old coaches. No caboose. Most trains had cabooses in those days because they carried a lot of brakemen. Had to have them to wrangle the hand brakes. Expect the brakeman the operator was talking to was the only one this train had. Expect that was why it was so late. I mean the railroad wasn't wasting any good equipment and any extra men on this train, and it was being shoved along slow when and as how between other trains.

I stood there shaking inside and the engine was wheezing some and the engineer and fireman were moving slow and tired around it, fussing with an oilcan and a tin of grease. That was the only sign of life I could see along the whole train. What light there was in the coaches, only one lantern lit in each, wasn't any stronger than the moonlight outside and that made the windows blank-like and I couldn't see through them. Except for the wheezing engine, that train was a tired and sleeping or dead thing on the track. Then I saw someone step down from the first coach and stretch and move into the moonlight. He was a soldier, a captain, and he looked tired and sleepy and disgusted with himself and the whole world. He pulled a cigar from a pocket and leaned against the side of the coach, lighting the cigar and blowing out smoke in a slow puff. Seeing him so lazy and casual, I stopped shaking and moved into the open and closer to the coach and shifted around trying to find an angle that would stop the light reflection on the windows and let me see in. Then I stopped still. The captain was looking at me. "Jee-sus," he said. "Why does everybody want to gawk at them? Even kids." He took a long drag on his cigar and blew a pair of fat smoke rings. "You must want to bad," he said. "Up so late. Go on in take a look." I stared at him, scared now two ways. I was scared to go in where those Indians were and scared not to, after he'd said I could and just about ordered I should. "Go ahead," he said. "They don't eat boys. Only girls. Only at lunchtime." And sudden I knew he was just making a tired joke, and it would be all right and I went up the steps to the front platform and peered in.

Indians. Fighting Indians. The fighting Nez Percés who had led United States soldiers a bloody chase through the mountains of three states. The big and fierce redmen who had fought many times their own number of better armed soldiers to a frequent standstill in the high passes. And they weren't big and they weren't fierce at all. They were huddled figures on the coach seats, two to a seat down the twin rows, braves and squaws and young ones alike, all dusty and tired and hunched together at the shoulders in drowsy silence or sprawled apart over the window sills and seat arms in sleep. In the dim light they looked exactly like the tame Indians I'd seen, and they seemed to shrink and shrivel even more as I looked at them and there was no room in me for any emotion but disappointment, and when I noticed the soldiers sleeping in the first seats close to me I sniffed to myself at the silly notion any guards might be needed on the train. There wasn't the slightest hint of danger anywhere around. Being on that train was no different from being off it except that it was being on a stopped train and not being outside on the ground. It didn't even take any particular nerve to do what I did when I started walking down the aisle.

The only way I know to describe it is that I was in a sort of trance of disappointment and I wanted to see everything and I went straight down the aisle looking all around me. And those Indians acted like I wasn't there at all. Those that were awake. Each of them had his eyes fixed somewhere, maybe out a window or at the floor or just at some point ahead, and didn't move them. They knew I was there. I could tell that. A feeling. A little crawling on my skin. But they wouldn't look at me. They were somehow off away in a place all their own and they weren't going to let me come near getting in there with them or let me know they even saw me outside of it. Except one. He was a young one, a boy like me only a couple of years younger, and he was scrooged down against a sleeping brave—maybe his father—and his small eyes, solid black in the dim light, looked at me, and his head turned slow to keep them on me as I went past and I could sense them on me as I went on till the back of the seat shut them off.

Still in that funny trance I went into the next coach and through it and to the third coach and on to the last. Each was the same. Soldiers slumped in sleep, and the huddled figures of the Indians in different pairings and sprawled positions but the effect the same and then at the end of the last car I saw him. He had a seat to himself and the headdress with its red-tipped feathers hung from the rack above the seat. He was asleep with an arm along the window sill, his head resting on it. I stopped and stared at him and the low light from the lantern near the end of the coach shone on the coppery texture of his face and the bare skin of his chest where it showed through the fallen-apart folds of the blanket wrapped around him. I stared at him and I felt cheated and empty inside. Even Jacob wasn't big or fierce. He wasn't as big as my father. He was short. Maybe broad and rather thick in the body but not much, even that way. And his face was quiet and— well, the only word I can ever think of is peaceful. I stared at him and then I started a little because he wasn't sleeping. One eyelid had twitched a bit. All at once I knew he was just pretending. He was pretending to be asleep so he wouldn't have to be so aware of the stares of anyone coming aboard to gawk at him. And sudden I felt ashamed and I hurried to the back platform to leave the train, and in the shadow there I stumbled over a sleeping soldier and heard him rousing himself as I scrambled down the steps.

That started what happened afterwards. Expect I'm really to blame for it all. Mean to say it probably wouldn't have happened if I hadn't been hurrying and wakened that soldier. He didn't know I was there. He was too full of sleep at first and didn't know what had awakened him. While I stayed in the dark shadow by the coach, afraid to go out into the moonlight, he stood up and stretched and came down the steps without noticing me and went around the end of the train toward the wider shadow on the other side, and as he went I saw him pulling a bottle out of a pocket. I felt safe again and started away and turned to look back, and the light was just right for me to see some movement inside through the window by the last seat. Jacob was standing up. All kinds of wild notions poured through my mind and I couldn't move and then he was emerging through the rear door on to the platform and I wasn't exactly scared because I wasn't conscious of feeling anything at all except that I couldn't move. Time seemed to hang there motionless around me. Then I realized he wasn't doing anything and wasn't going to do anything. He wasn't even aware of me or if he was I was without meaning for him and he had seen me and dismissed me. He was standing quiet by the rear railing and his blanket was left inside and the cold night air was blowing against his bare chest above his leather breeches but he didn't appear to notice that. He was looking back along the double iron line of the track toward the tiny point of light that was my father's lantern by the west switch. He stood there, still and quiet, and I stayed where I was and watched him and he did not move and stood there looking far along the westward track and that was what we were doing, Jacob and I, when the soldier came back around the end of the train.

Thinking about it later I couldn't blame that soldier too much. Maybe had orders to keep the Indians in their seats or not let them on the rear platform or something like that. Probably was worried about drinking on duty and not wanting to be caught letting anything slip with the tang plain on his breath. Could be too he'd taken on more than he could handle right. Anyway he was surprised and mad when he saw Jacob standing there. He reached first and pulled some object off the platform floor and when he had it I could see it was his rifle. Then he jumped up the steps and started prodding Jacob with the rifle barrel toward the door. Jacob looked at him once and away and turned slow and started to move and the soldier must have thought Jacob moved too slow because he swung the gun around to use the stock end like a club and smack Jacob on the back. I couldn't see exactly what happened then because the scuffle was too sudden and quick but there was a blur of movement and the soldier came tumbling off the platform to the ground near me and the gun landed beside him. He was so mad he tripped all over himself getting to his feet and scrabbling for the gun and he whipped it up and hip-aimed it at Jacob and tried to fire it and the breech mechanism jammed some way and he clawed at it to make it work.

And Jacob stood there on the platform, still and quiet again, looking down at the soldier with bare breast broadside to the gun. I could see his eyes bright and black in the moonlight and the shining on the coppery firmness of his face and he did not move and of a sudden I realized he was waiting. He was waiting for the bullet. He was expecting it and waiting for it and he would not move. And I jumped forward and grabbed the rifle barrel and pulled hard on it. "No," I shouted. "Not like that." And the soldier stumbled and fell against me and both of us went down and someone was yelling at us and when I managed to get to my feet I saw it was the captain and the soldier was up too, standing stiff and awkward at attention. "Bloody Indian," the soldier said. "Trying to get away." The captain looked up and saw Jacob standing there and jerked a bit with recognizing who it was. "He was not," I said. "He was just standing there." The captain looked at the soldier and shook his head slow. "Jee-sus," he said. "You'd have shot that one." The captain shook his head again like he was disgusted and tired of everything and maybe even of living. "What's the use," he said. He flipped a thumb at the soldier. "Pick up your gun and get on forward." The soldier hurried off and the captain looked at Jacob and Jacob looked down at him, still and quiet and not moving a muscle. "There's fools of every color," the captain said and Jacob's eyes brightened a little as if he understood and I expect he did because I'd heard he could speak English when he wanted to. The captain wiped a hand across his face. "Stand on that damned platform as long as you want," he said. He remembered he had a cigar in his other hand and looked at it and it was out and he threw it on the ground and swung around and went toward the front of the train again, and I wanted to follow him but I couldn't because now Jacob was looking at me.

He looked down at me what seemed a long time and then he motioned at me and I could tell he wanted me to step out further into the moonlight. I did and he leaned forward to peer at me. He reached a hand out toward me, palm flat and down, and said something in his own language and for a moment I was there with him in the world that was different and beyond my own everyday world and then he swung away and stepped to stand by the rear railing again and I knew I was outside again, outside of his mind and put away and no more to him than any other object around. He was alone there looking far down the track and it sank slow and deep in me that he was looking far past the tiny light point of my father's lantern, far on where the lone track ran straight along the slow-rising reaches of distance into the horizon that led past the longest vision at last to the great climbing mountains. He was looking back along the iron trail that was taking him and his children away from a valley that would make a man want to put his feet firm on the earth and stretch tall and was taking them to an unknown place where they would not be themselves any longer but only some among many of many tribes and tongues and all dependent on the bounty of a forgetful government. It wasn't an Indian I was seeing there any more. It was a man. It wasn't Jacob, the tamed chief that even foolish kids could gawk at. It was Mountain Elk, the Big-Deer-That-Walks-the-High-Places and he was big, really big, and he was one meant to walk the high places.

He stood there looking down the track and the westbound night freight came rumbling out of the east and strained past, and he stood there watching it go westward along the track and his train began to move, creeping eastward slow and feeling forward, and I watched it go and long as I could see him he was standing there, still and quiet, looking straight out along the back trail.

Well. I've taken you to where I was headed. It's only a hop now to those moccasins. I tried to tell the other boys about it the next day and likely boasted and strutted in the telling and they wouldn't believe me. Oh, they'd believe I saw the Indians all right. Had to. The telegraph operator backed my saying I was there. Even that I went aboard. But they wouldn't believe the rest. And because they wouldn't believe me I had to keep pounding it at them, telling it over and over. Expect I was getting to be mighty unpopular. But Jacob saved me even though I never saw him again. There was a day a bunch of us boys were playing some game or other back of the telegraph shack and sudden we realized someone had come up from somewhere and was watching us. An Indian. Seemed to be just an ordinary everyday sort of tame Indian. But he was looking us over intent and careful and he picked me and came straight to me. He put out a hand, palm flat and down, and said something to me in his Indian talk and pointed far off to the east and south and back again to me and reached inside the old blanket he had fastened around him with a belt and took out a dirty cloth-wrapped package and laid it at my feet and went away and faded out of sight around the shack. When I unrolled that package there were these moccasins.

Funny thing. I never wanted to go around telling my story to the other boys again. Didn't need to. Whether they believed or not wasn't important any more. I had those moccasins. In a way they made me one of Jacob's children. Remembering that has helped me sometimes in tough spots.

Jack Schaefer comments on "Jacob"

It may be polite but it is also somewhat silly to ask a writer (my kind anyway) to talk about a story he has written. If the story is any good, what he had to say has already been said. And he is probably the last person to be able to assess with reasonable accuracy what he did in the writing. Caught up in the creative process, he was aware only of what he wanted to do, not of what he managed to accomplish.

Moreover, he was not even particularly aware of techniques in the writing. He simply "saw" a story in his mind, a sequence of events which had some meaning for him, and went ahead and told it in a manner which "sounded" or "felt" right to him. Only when he was finished, could he look back over it and (if there were any reason for such nonsense) begin to recognize and to label the methods and devices he used. Even then, to be honest, he would have to admit that often his reason for doing this or that had been different from what some critic or teacher might cite for it.

What I am doing now is looking back over two of my stories and being fool enough to prattle about them. I will touch on when and why they were written and their original publication because such background data, when available, sometimes adds interest to study of a story and can aid in interpretation of it. I will mention, too, some aspects of these two and their writing about which, if I were the teacher, I would attempt to stir discussion and, hopefully, debate among my students.

"Jacob" was written so long ago (my notebook says in 1950) that my memory of the writing is flimsy. Obviously I was already well on my way to my now confirmed conviction that in some respects in the conquest and settlement of the United States the Indians were the civilized inhabitants and we whites the invading barbarians. Probably I started with the nebulous notion of writing a story in which someone would discover the interesting fact, rarely recognized at the time, that Indians were not only people but often admirable ones. Obviously, too, I had been reading about Chief Joseph of the Nez Percé. Jacob, of course, is Chief Joseph. Since I was writing fiction, creating my own imagined situation, I changed his name. Some readers have an irritating habit of inditing indignant letters to a writer who uses a specific historical character and slips on any last least tiny detail.

Why is the story called "Jacob" when it is not about Jacob but about a boy and what he learns from a brief association with Jacob?

Is that because Jacob is the key character, the pivotal one in the plot? No. He is not the key character. The boy is. But I have always had a fondness for using the names of characters for titles. The boy had no name. Jacob did.

Knox Burger, then the fiction editor of *Collier's* who had been publishing some of my stories, promptly rejected this one. "The atmosphere," he wrote my agent, "is very convincing, but I just don't think readers will hold still for all this narration." I recall being annoyed. It seemed to me that all the narration was necessary to achieve the effect I wanted. Whether Burger's verdict would have been echoed by other magazine editors remains unknown. My book publishers were preparing for the presses a short novel of mine and wanted to fatten the volume a bit. They added "Jacob" to it.

The story is written in the first person, told by the boy himself. Why? Because that "felt" right. Why did it feel right? Probably because this was to be a record of a personal experience—of an *interior* experience, not just what the boy did and saw and heard, but what happened in his mind and being. Well, then, why didn't I use one of the popular methods of the serious long-haired psychology-addicted writers who use third-person narration, then crawl down inside the minds of their characters and explain what goes on there? I simply do not like that method. I prefer to have characters speak for themselves, reveal by their words and actions what goes on in their minds, instead of having that spelled out for me. Even when I do use the third-person approach, I try to present and to develop my characters and to show whatever changes may take place in them primarily through what they do and say—in a series of hints and clues for readers to grasp and interpret for themselves. But no such reasoning intruded when I chose the first person in this case. It merely felt right.

The style in "Jacob" has its own peculiarities. At the start it is distinctly colloquial, an attempt to give the impression of one person talking directly to another. The favorite device is elliptical sentences —which is the way most of us talk most of the time. The commonest trick used is a dropping of subjects, a jumping right into sentences with the predicates—which is a prevalent habit of old-time western-ers when telling a tale. Was I conscious of deliberately using such tricks? No. I had imagined the narrator, thought about him long enough (this process sometimes takes longer than the actual writing) to know him very well, then was letting him talk through me and my typewriter.

As the story progresses, this narrator becomes more lit'ry. His sentences lengthen, are less elliptical, edge more towards purple prose, particularly in the sections where "all this narration" is striving for unobtrusive emotional response. When the narrator catches himself and interpolates something, he is usually more colloquial again. Was I aware of doing that? No. I was aware only that I was aiming as I went along at the portions which meant most to me. Probably I let myself go more when I hit those.

The father is an only-good-Indian-is-a-dead-Indian fanatic. Why? Not just because that was the attitude of so many settlers in the West. The father provides the background of prejudice which the boy has absorbed and which Jacob will overcome for him. On the other hand the captain, in his brief appearance, is more tolerant, more understanding. Is that for contrast, to fill in the general picture a bit more? Perhaps it is. Would his attitude have some impact on the boy? Perhaps it does. Would he need to be a tolerant, patient, even kindly man to be the kind who would not only let the boy board the train but even urge him into it? I suppose he would. But no such reasoning nagged me. In my reading of military journals of the Indian wars I had noted that some soldiers, particularly officers, developed a reluctant admiration for their redskin opponents. I was merely paying my respects to such officers.

Moccasins. Why begin and end with a pair of moccasins? They are the most transparent device of all—and easily the most important. They provide the excuse for the narrator to start his story—which is convenient but only incidental. They take him back to his boyhood. The significant word there is "back." The narrator is not a boy, could not possibly be a boy. He is a man, probably middle-aged, telling about something which happened when he was a boy. The added time dimension is vital. No boy could understand and talk about the Jacob experience as this man does after the years have given him perspective on it. And the point, the purpose of "all this narration" is not just to present what the boy learned about Indians in general and Jacob in particular—it is the impact that learning had upon his whole life. The story was written, as most of mine are, for the last paragraph—for the last two sentences. I am one of those writers afflicted with a need to know the finish, the goal, the final impression I hope to leave, usually as in this case the exact ending, before I can write even a first sentence.

And those moccasins "package" the story. They wrap it up, hold it together, give it a beginning and an ending, help make it what I like to think is an artistic whole. They sound the motif at the start—and they hearken back to it at the finish.

It would be a waste of time, I believe, for any teacher who might someday be teaching "Jacob" to go into the techniques involved any further than I have done in the preceding paragraphs: a bit about the use of a narrator, about the style, about the concise combination of characters, about the moccasin device for shaping the narrative. "Jacob" is basically a simple direct story. Simple in structure, direct (except for the time jump at the start and the end) in movement. If it has any value beyond that of telling a tale that may have some interest inherent in the events themselves, such value comes from the totality of it, from the overall effect.

Does "Jacob" achieve its purpose of creating in the reader more sympathy for and greater recognition of Indians as fellow human beings—of, perhaps, giving more insight into the relationship between whites and Indians in the opening days of the American West? Could the same purpose have been achieved, perhaps better achieved, without "all this narration"? What exactly did the boy-man learn about Indians in general and Jacob in particular? Simply that they were people too? The writer himself insists that the real point of the story is not just what the boy learned but the impact that had upon his own life. Yet he never once describes that boy-man, merely lets him talk. Does the talking reveal in any way what kind of a human being that boy-man is in himself, offer any hints of what kind of a person Jacob has helped him become?

I would like to be a fly on the classroom wall and hear the answers students might give to such questions.

Stubby Pringle's Christmas

Jack Schaefer

High on the mountainside by the little line cabin in the crisp clean dusk of evening Stubby Pringle swings into saddle. He has shape of bear in the dimness, bundled thick against cold. Double socks crowd scarred boots. Leather chaps with hair out cover patched corduroy pants. Fleece-lined jacket with wear of winters on it bulges body and heavy gloves blunt fingers. Two gay red bandannas folded together fatten throat under chin. Battered hat is pulled down to sit on ears and in side pocket of jacket are rabbit-skin earmuffs he can put to use if he needs them.

Stubby Pringle swings up into saddle. He looks out and down over worlds of snow and ice and tree and rock. He spreads arms wide and they embrace whole ranges of hills. He stretches tall and hat brushes stars in sky. He is Stubby Pringle, cowhand of the Triple X, and this is his night to howl. He is Stubby Pringle, son of the wild jackass, and he is heading for the Christmas dance at the schoolhouse in the valley.

Stubby Pringle swings up and his horse stands like rock. This is the pride of his string, flop-eared ewe-necked cat-hipped strawberry roan that looks like it should have died weeks ago but has iron rods for bones and nitroglycerin for blood and can go from here to doomsday with nothing more than mouthfuls of snow for water and tufts of winter-cured bunch-grass snatched between drifts for food. It stands like rock. It knows the folly of trying to unseat Stubby. It wastes no energy in futile explosions. It knows that twenty-seven miles of hard winter going are foreordained for this evening and twenty-seven more of harder uphill return by morning. It has done this before. It is saving the dynamite under its hide for the destiny of a true cowpony which is to take its rider where he wants to go—and bring him back again.

Stubby Pringle sits his saddle and he grins into cold and distance and future full of festivity. Join me in a look at what can be seen of him despite the bundling and frosty breath vapor that soon will hang icicles on his nose. Those are careless haphazard scrambled features under the low hat-brim, about as handsome as a blue boar's snout. Not much fuzz yet on his chin. Why, shucks, is he just a boy? Don't make that mistake, though his twentieth birthday is still six weeks away. Don't make the mistake Hutch Handley made last summer when he thought this was young unseasoned stuff and took to ragging Stubby and wound up with ears pinned back and upper lip split and nose mashed flat and the whole of him dumped in a rain-barrel. Stubby has been taking care of himself since he was orphaned at thirteen. Stubby has been doing man's work since he was fifteen. Do you think Hardrock Harper of the Triple X would have anything but an all-around hard-proved hand up here at his farthest winter line camp siding Old Jake Hanlon, toughest hard-bitten old cowman ever to ride range?

Stubby Pringle slips gloved hand under rump to wipe frost off the sad-dle. No sense letting it melt into patches of corduroy pants. He slaps right-side saddlebag. It contains a burlap bag wrapped around a two-pound box of candy, of fancy chocolates with variegated interiors he acquired two months ago and has kept hidden from Old Jake. He slaps leftside saddle-bag. It holds a burlap bag wrapped around a paper parcel that contains a close-folded piece of dress goods and a roll of pink ribbon. Interesting items, yes. They are ammunition for the campaign he has in mind to soften the affections of whichever female of the right vintage among those at the schoolhouse appeals to him most and seems most susceptible.

Stubby Pringle settles himself firmly into the saddle. He is just another of far-scattered poorly-paid patched-clothes cowhands that inhabit these parts and likely marks and smells of his calling have not all been scrubbed away. He knows that. But this is his night to howl. He is Stubby Pringle, true-begotten son of the wildest jackass, and he has been riding line through hell and highwater and winter storms for two months without a break and he has done his share of the work and more than his share because Old Jake is getting along and slowing some and this is his night to stomp floor-boards till schoolhouse shakes and kick heels up to lanterns above and whirl a willing female till she is dizzy enough to see past patched clothes to the man inside them. He wriggles toes deep into stirrups and settles himself firmly in the saddle.

"I could of et them choc'lates," says Old Jake from the cabin doorway. "They wasn't hid good," he says. "No good at all."

"An' be beat like a drum," says Stubby. "An' wrung out like a dirty dishrag."

"By who?" says Old Jake. "By a young un like you? Why, I'd of tied you in knots afore you knew what's what iffen you tried it. You're a dang-blatted young fool," he says. "A ding-busted dang-blatted fool. Riding out a night like this iffen it is Chris'mas eve. A dong-bonging ding-busted dang-blatted fool," he says. "But iffen I was your age agin, I reckon I'd be doing it too." He cackles like an old rooster. "Squeeze one of 'em for me," he says and he steps back inside and he closes the door.

Stubby Pringle is alone out there in the darkening dusk, alone with flop-eared ewe-necked cat-hipped roan that can go to the last trumpet call under him and with cold of wicked winter wind around him and with twenty-seven miles of snow-dumped distance ahead of him. "Wahoo!" he yells. "Skip to my Loo!" he shouts. "Do-si-do and round about!"

He lifts reins and the roan sighs and lifts feet. At easy warming-up amble they drop over the edge of benchland where the cabin snugs into tall pines and on down the great bleak expanse of mountainside.

Stubby Pringle, spurs a jingle, jogs upslope through crusted snow. The roan, warmed through, moves strong and steady under him. Line cabin and line work are far forgotten things back and back and up and up the mighty mass of mountain. He is Stubby Pringle, rooting tooting hard-working hard-playing cowhand of the Triple X, heading for the Christmas dance at the schoolhouse in the valley.

He tops out on one of the lower ridges. He pulls rein to give the roan a breather. He brushes an icicle off his nose. He leans forward and reaches to brush several more off sidebars of old bit in the bridle. He straightens tall. Far ahead, over top of last and lowest ridge, on into the valley, he can see tiny specks of glowing allure that are schoolhouse windows. Lights and gaiety and good liquor and fluttering skirts are there. "Wahoo!" he yells. "Gals an' women an' grandmothers!" he shouts. "Raise your skirts and start askipping! I'm acoming!"

He slaps spurs to roan. It leaps like mountain lion, out and down, full into hard gallop downslope, rushing, reckless of crusted drifts and ice-coated bush-branches slapping at them. He is Stubby Pringle, born with spurs on, nursed on tarantula juice, weaned on rawhide, at home in the saddle of a hurricane in shape of horse that can race to outer edge of eternity and back, heading now for high-jinks two months overdue. He is ten feet tall and the horse is gigantic, with wings, iron-boned and dynamite-fueled, soaring in forty-foot leaps down the flank of the whitened wonder of a winter world.

They slow at the bottom. They stop. They look up the rise of the last low ridge ahead. The roan paws frozen ground and snorts twin plumes of

frosty vapor. Stubby reaches around to pull down fleece-lined jacket that
has worked a bit up back. He pats rightside saddlebag. He pats leftside
saddlebag. He lifts reins to soar up and over last low ridge.

Hold it, Stubby. What is that? Off to the right.

He listens. He has ears that can catch snitch of mouse chewing on
chunk of bacon rind beyond the log wall by his bunk. He hears. Sound of
ax striking wood.

What kind of dong-bonging ding-busted dang-blatted fool would be
chopping wood on a night like this and on Christmas Eve and with a dance
underway at the schoolhouse in the valley? What kind of chopping is this
anyway? Uneven in rhythm, feeble in stroke. Trust Stubby Pringle, who
has chopped wood enough for cookstove and fireplace to fill a long freight
train, to know how an ax should be handled.

There. That does it. That whopping sound can only mean that the
blade has hit at an angle and bounced away without biting. Some dong-
bonged ding-busted dang-blatted fool is going to be cutting off some of
his own toes.

He pulls the roan around to the right. He is Stubby Pringle, born to
tune of bawling bulls and blatting calves, branded at birth, cowman raised
and cowman to the marrow, and no true cowman rides on without stopping
to check anything strange on range. Roan chomps on bit, annoyed at inter-
ruption. It remembers who is in saddle. It sighs and obeys. They move
quietly in dark of night past boles of trees jet black against dim greyness of
crusted snow on ground. Light shows faintly ahead. Lantern light through
a small oiled-paper window.

Yes. Of course. Just where it has been for eight months now. The
Henderson place. Man and woman and small girl and waist-high boy.
Homesteaders. Not even fools, homesteaders. Worse than that. Out of their
minds altogether. All of them. Out here anyway. Betting the government
they can stave off starving for five years in exchange for one hundred sixty
acres of land. Land that just might be able to support seven jack-rabbits
and two coyotes and nine rattlesnakes and maybe all of four thin steers to
a whole section. In a good year. Homesteaders. Always out of almost everything, money and food and tools and smiles and joy of living. Everything.
Except maybe hope and stubborn endurance.

Stubby Pringle nudges the reluctant roan along. In patch-light from the
window by a tangled pile of dead tree branches he sees a woman. Her face
is grey and pinched and tired. An old stocking-cap is pulled down on her
head. Ragged man's jacket bumps over long woolsey dress and clogs arms
as she tries to swing an ax into a good-sized branch on the ground.

Whopping sound and ax bounces and barely misses an ankle.

"Quit that!" says Stubby, sharp. He swings the roan in close. He looks
down at her. She drops ax and backs away, frightened. She is ready to bolt
into two-room bark-slab shack. She looks up. She sees that haphazard
scrambled features under low hatbrim are crinkled in what could be a grin.
She relaxes some, hand on door latch.

"Ma'am," says Stubby. "You trying to cripple yourself?" She just stares
at him. "Man's work," he says. "Where's your man?"

"Inside," she says; then, quick, "He's sick."

"Bad?" says Stubby.

"Was," she says. "Doctor that was here this morning thinks he'll be all right now. Only he's almighty weak. All wobbly. Sleeps most of the time."

"Sleeps," says Stubby, indignant. "When there's wood to be chopped."

"He's been almighty tired," she says, quick, defensive. "Even afore he was took sick. Wore out." She is rubbing cold hands together, trying to warm them. "He tried," she says, proud. "Only a while ago. Couldn't even get his pants on. Just fell flat on the floor."

Stubby looks down at her. "An' you ain't tired?" he says.

"I ain't got time to be tired," she says. "Not with all I got to do."

Stubby Pringle looks off past dark boles of trees at last row ridgetop that hides valley and schoolhouse. "I reckon I could spare a bit of time," he says. "Likely they ain't much more'n started yet," he says. He looks again at the woman. He sees grey pinched face. He sees cold-shivering under bumpy jacket. "Ma'am," he says. "Get on in there an' warm your gizzard some. I'll just chop you a bit of wood."

Roan stands with dropping reins, ground-tied, disgusted. It shakes head to send icicles tinkling from bit and bridle. Stopped in midst of epic run, wind-eating, mile-gobbling, iron-boned and dynamite-fueled, and for what? For silly chore of chopping.

Fifteen feet away Stubby Pringle chops wood. Moon is rising over last low ridgetop and its light, filtered through trees, shines on leaping blade. He is Stubby Pringle, moonstruck maverick of the Triple X, born with ax in hands, with strength of stroke in muscles, weaned on whetstone, fed on cordwood, raised to fell whole forests. He is ten feet tall and ax is enormous in moonlight and chips fly like stormflakes of snow and blade slices through branches thick as his arm, through logs thick as his thigh.

He leans ax against a stump and he spreads arms wide and he scoops up whole cords at a time and strides to door and kicks it open . . .

Both corners of front room by fireplace are piled full now, floor to ceiling, good wood, stout wood, seasoned wood, wood enough for a whole wicked winter week. Chore done and done right, Stubby looks around him. Fire is burning bright and well-fed, working on warmth. Man lies on big old bed along opposite wall, blanket over, eyes closed, face grey-pale, snoring long and slow. Woman fusses with something at old woodstove. Stubby steps to doorway to back-room. He pulls aside hanging cloth. Faint in dimness inside he sees two low bunks and in one, under an old quilt, a curly-headed small girl and in the other, under other old quilt, a boy who would be waist-high awake and standing. He sees them still and quiet, sleeping sound. "Cute little devils," he says.

He turns back and the woman is coming toward him, cup of coffee in hand, strong and hot and steaming. Coffee the kind to warm the throat and gizzard of chore-doing hard-chopping cowhand on a cold cold night. He takes the cup and raises it to his lips. Drains it in two gulps. "Thank you, ma'am," he says. "That was right kindly of you." He sets cup on table. "I got to be getting along," he says. He starts toward outer door.

He stops, hand on door latch. Something is missing in two-room shack. Trust Stubby Pringle to know what. "Where's your tree?" he says. "Kids got to have a Christmas tree."

He sees the woman sink down on chair. He hears a sigh come from her. "I ain't had time to cut one," she says.

"I reckon not," says Stubby. "Man's job anyway," he says. "I'll get it for you. Won't take a minute. Then I got to be going."

He strides out. He scoops up ax and strides off, upslope some where small pines climb. He stretches tall and his legs lengthen and he towers huge among trees swinging with ten-foot steps. He is Stubby Pringle, born an expert on Christmas trees, nursed on pine needles, weaned on pine cones, raised with an eye for size and shape and symmetry. There. A beauty. Perfect. Grown for this and for nothing else. Ax blade slices keen and swift. Tree topples. He strides back with tree on shoulder. He rips leather whangs from his saddle and lashes two pieces of wood to tree bottom, crosswise, so tree can stand upright again.

Stubby Pringle strides into shack, carrying tree. He sets it up, center of front-room floor, and it stands straight, trim and straight, perky and proud and pointed. "There you are, ma'am," he says. "Get your things out an' start decorating. I got to be going." He moves toward outer door.

He stops in outer doorway. He hears the sigh behind him. "We got no things," she says. "I was figuring to buy some but sickness took the money."

Stubby Pringle looks off at last low ridgetop hiding valley and schoolhouse. "Reckon I still got a bit of time," he says. "They'll be whooping it mighty late." He turns back, closing door. He sheds hat and gloves and bandannas and jacket. He moves about checking everything in the sparse front room. He asks for things and the woman jumps to get those few of them she has. He tells her what to do and she does. He does plenty himself. With this and with that magic wonders arrive. He is Stubby Pringle, born to poverty and hard work, weaned on nothing, fed on less, raised to make do with least possible and make the most of that. Pinto beans strung on thread brighten tree in firelight and lantern light like strings of store-bought beads. Strips of one bandanna, cut with shears from sewing-box, bob in bows on branch-ends like gay red flowers. Snippets of fleece from jacket-lining sprinkled over tree glisten like fresh fall of snow. Miracles flow from strong blunt fingers through bits of old paper-bags and dabs of flour paste into link chains and twisted small streamers and two jaunty little hats and two smart little boats with sails.

"Got to finish it right," says Stubby Pringle. From strong blunt fingers comes five-pointed star, triple-thickness to make it stiff, twisted bit of old wire to hold it upright. He fastens this to topmost tip of topmost bough. He wraps lone bandanna left around throat and jams battered hat on head and shrugs into now-skimpy-lined jacket. "A right nice little tree," he says. "All you got to do now is get out what you got for the kids and put it under. I really got to be going." He starts toward outer door.

He stops in open doorway. He hears the sigh behind him. He knows without looking around the woman has slumped into old rocking chair.

"We ain't got anything for them," she says. "Only now this tree. Which I don't mean it isn't a fine grand tree. It's more'n we'd of had 'cept for you."

Stubby Pringle stands in open doorway looking out into cold clean moonlit night. Somehow he knows without turning head two tears are sliding down thin pinched cheeks. "You go on along," she says. "They're good young uns. They know how it is. They ain't expecting a thing."

Stubby Pringle stands in open doorway looking out at last ridgetop that hides valley and schoolhouse. "All the more reason," he says soft to himself. "All the more reason something should be there when they wake." He sighs too. "I'm a dong-bonging ding-busted dang-blatted fool," he says. "But I reckon I still got a mite more time. Likely they'll be sashaying around till it's most morning."

Stubby Pringle strides on out, leaving door open. He strides back, closing door with heel behind him. In one hand he has burlap bag wrapped around paper parcel. In other hand he has squarish chunk of good pine wood. He tosses bag-parcel into lap-folds of woman's apron.

"Unwrap it," he says. "There's the makings for a right cute dress for the girl. Needle-and-threader like you can whip it up in no time. I'll just whittle me out a little something for the boy."

Moon is high in cold cold sky. Frosty clouds drift up there with it. Tiny flakes of snow float through upper air. Down below by a two-room shack droops a disgusted cowpony roan, ground-tied, drooping like statue snow-crusted. It is accepting the inescapable destiny of its kind which is to wait for its rider, to conserve deep-bottomed dynamite energy, to be ready to race to the last margin of motion when waiting is done.

Inside the shack fire in fireplace cheerily gobbles wood, good wood, stout wood, seasoned wood, warming two-rooms well. Man lies on bed, turned on side, curled up some, snoring slow and steady. Woman sits in rocking chair, sewing. Her head nods slow and drowsy and her eyelids sag weary but her fingers fly, stitch-stitch-stitch. A dress has shaped under her hands, small and flounced and with little puff-sleeves, fine dress, fancy dress, dress for smiles and joy of living. She is sewing pink ribbon around collar and down front and into fluffy bow on back.

On a stool nearby sits Stubby Pringle, piece of good pine wood in one hand, knife in other hand, fine knife, splendid knife, all-around-accomplished knife, knife he always has with him, seven-bladed knife with four for cutting from little to big and corkscrew and can opener and screwdriver. Big cutting blade has done its work. Little cutting blade is in use now. He is Stubby Pringle, born with feel for knives in hand, weaned on emery wheel, fed on shavings, raised to whittle his way through the world. Tiny chips fly and shavings flutter. There in his hands, out of good pine wood, something is shaping. A horse. Yes. Flop-eared ewe-necked cat-hipped horse. Flop-eared head is high on ewe neck, stretched out, sniffing wind, snorting into distance. Cat-hips are hunched forward, caught in crouch for forward leap. It is a horse fit to carry a waist-high boy to uttermost edge of eternity and back.

Stubby Pringle carves swift and sure. Little cutting blade makes final little cutting snitches. Yes. Tiny mottlings and markings make no mistaking. It is a strawberry roan. He closes knife and puts it in pocket. He looks up. Dress is finished in woman's lap. But woman's head has dropped down in exhaustion. She sits slumped deep in rocking chair and she too snores slow and steady.

Stubby Pringle stands up. He takes dress and puts it under tree, fine dress, fancy dress, dress waiting now for small girl to wake and wear it with smiles and joy of living. He sets wooden horse beside it, fine horse, proud horse, snorting-into-distance horse, cat-hips crouched, waiting now for waist-high boy to wake and ride it around the world.

Quietly he piles wood on fire and banks ashes around to hold it for morning. Quietly he pulls on hat and wraps bandanna around and shrugs into skimpy-lined jacket. He looks at old rocking chair and tired woman slumped in it. He strides to outer door and out, leaving door open. He strides back, closing door with heel behind. He carries other burlap bag wrapped around box of candy, of fine chocolates, fancy chocolates with variegated interiors. Gently he lays this in lap of woman. Gently he takes big old shawl from wall nail and lays this over her. He stands by big old bed and looks down at snoring man. "Poor devil," he says. "Ain't fair to forget him." He takes knife from pocket, fine knife, seven-bladed knife, and lays this on blanket on bed. He picks up gloves and blows out lantern and swift as sliding moon shadow he is gone.

High high up frosty clouds scuttle across face of moon. Wind whips through topmost tips of tall pines. What is it that hurtles like hurricane far down there on upslope of last low ridge, scattering drifts, smashing through brush, snorting defiance at distance? It is flop-eared ewe-necked cat-hipped roan, iron boned and dynamite fueled, ramming full gallop through the dark of night. Firm in saddle is Stubby Pringle, spurs ajingle, toes atingle, out on prowl, ready to howl, heading for the dance at the schoolhouse in the valley. He is ten feet tall, great as a grizzly, and the roan is gigantic, with wings, soaring upward in thirty-foot leaps. They top out and roan rears high, pawing stars out of sky, and drops down, cat-hips hunched for fresh leap out and down.

Hold it, Stubby. Hold hard on reins. Do you see what is happening on out there in the valley?

Tiny lights that are schoolhouse windows are winking out. Tiny dark shapes moving about are horsemen riding off, are wagons pulling away.

Moon is dropping down the sky, haloed in frosty mist. Dark grey clouds dip and swoop around sweep of horizon. Cold winds weave rustling through ice-coated bushes and trees. What is that moving slow and lonesome up snow-covered mountainside? It is a flop-eared ewe-necked cat-hipped roan, just that, nothing more, small cowpony, worn and weary, taking its rider back to clammy bunk in cold line cabin. Slumped in saddle is Stubby Pringle, head down, shoulders sagged. He is just another of far-scattered poorly-paid patched-clothes cowhands who inhabit these parts. Just that. And something more. He is the biggest thing there is in the whole wide roster of the human race. He is a man who has given of himself, of what little he has and is, to bring smiles and joy of living to others along his way.

He jogs along, slump-sagged in saddle, thinking of none of this. He is thinking of dances undanced, of floorboards unstomped, of willing women left unwhirled.

He jogs along, half-asleep in saddle, and he is thinking now of bygone Christmas seasons and of a boy born to poverty and hard work and make-do poring in flicker of firelight over ragged old Christmas picturebook. And suddenly he hears something. The tinkle of sleigh bells.

Sleigh bells?

Yes. I am telling this straight. He and roan are weaving through thick-clumped brush. Winds are sighing high overhead and on up the mountainside and lower down here they are whipping mists and snow flurries all around him. He can see nothing in mystic moving dimness. But he can hear. The tinkle of sleigh bells, faint but clear, ghostly but unmistakable. And suddenly he sees something. Movement off to the left. Swift as wind, glimmers only through brush and mist and whirling snow, but unmistakable again. Antlered heads high, frosty breath streaming, bodies rushing swift and silent, floating in flash of movement past, seeming to leap in air alone needing no touch of ground beneath. Reindeer? Yes. Reindeer strong and silent and fleet out ot some far frozen northland marked on no map. Reindeer swooping down and leaping past and rising again and away, strong and effortless and fleeting. And with them, hard on their heels, almost lost in swirling snow mist of their passing, vague and formless but there, something big and bulky with runners like sleigh and flash of white beard whipping in wind and crack of long whip snapping.

Startled roan has seen something too. It stands rigid, head up, staring left and forward. Stubby Pringle, body atingle, stares too. Out of dark of night ahead, mingled with moan of wind, comes a long-drawn chuckle, deep deep chuckle, jolly and cheery and full of smiles and joy of living. And with it long-drawn words.

We-e-e-l-l-l do-o-o-ne . . . pa-a-a-artner!

Stubby Pringle shakes his head. He brushes an icicle from his nose. "An' I didn't have a single drink" he says. "Only coffee an' can't count that. Reckon I'm getting soft in the head." But he is cowman through and through, cowman through to the marrow. He can't ride on without stopping to check anything strange on his range. He swings down and leads off to the left. He fumbles in jacket pocket and finds a match. Strikes it. Holds it cupped and bends down. There they are. Unmistakable. Reindeer tracks.

Stubby Pringle stretches up tall. Stubby Pringle swings into saddle. Roan needs no slap of spurs to unleash strength in upward surge, up up up steep mountainside. It knows. There in saddle once more is Stubby Pringle, moonstruck maverick of the Triple X, all-around hard-proved hard-honed cowhand, ten feet tall, needing horse gigantic, with wings, iron-boned and dynamite-fueled, to take him home to little line cabin and some few winks of sleep before another day's hard work . . .

Stubby Pringle slips into cold clammy bunk. He wriggles vigorous to warm blanket under and blanket over.

"Was it worth all that riding?" comes voice of Old Jake Hanlon from other bunk on other wall.

"Why, sure," says Stubby. "I had me a right good time."

All right, now. Say anything you want. I know, you know, any dong-bonged ding-busted dang-blatted fool ought to know, that icicles breaking off branches can sound to drowsy ears something like sleigh bells. That blurry eyes half-asleep can see strange things. That deer and elk make tracks like those of reindeer. That wind sighing and soughing and moaning and maundering down mountains and through piny treetops can sound like someone shaping words. But we could talk and talk and it would mean nothing to Stubby Pringle.

Stubby is wiser than we are. He knows, he will always know, who it was, plump and jolly and belly-bouncing, that spoke to him that night out on wind-whipped winter-worn mountainside.

We-e-e-l-l-l do-o-o-ne . . . pa-a-a-rt-ner!

Jack Schaefer comments on "Stubby Pringle's Christmas"

In the relatively short time "Stubby Pringle's Christmas" has been in print it has met a mixed reception. Reviewers are rarely indifferent—they are usually strongly against it or equally strongly for it. Those against call it saccharine, sentimental, old-fashioned in the style of O. Henry or Bret Harte. They may be right in general judgment, but they have forgotten whatever they once knew of O. Henry and Bret Harte. Those for it pile up adjectives in praise and assert it is a fine blend of two forms, the Christmas story and the tall tale. It is a Christmas story. But it is not a tall tale. There is a brushing-in of tall-tale flavor, but the tale itself is not tall.

I doubt whether this is really a successful story. Personally I like it—but I can see why it annoys some critics. It is mannered, perhaps too mannered, tricky in style—with the tricks sticking out perhaps too far—and it *is* sentimental. Being sentimental is a crime to modern sophisticates. But bad or good, "Stubby" can be regarded as a fair example of one thing: a professional writer doing a job he was asked to do and trying to have fun in the doing.

In the summer of 1963 *Boys' Life,* which like other magazines usually works six or more months ahead of schedule, asked me to pinch-hit for someone who was ill and supply a Christmas story for the December issue. In warm sunny weather I started fishing for a story idea which quite likely would end up full of wintry weather. No luck—not because of the weather but probably because I was out of practice, had stopped writing short stories some years before in response to the dwindling of one-time markets. Then I happened to come on an old back-number of *Montana,* magazine of the Montana Historical Society. The cover carried a reproduction of a Charley Russell painting. A grizzled time-worn tough-looking cowboy bundled up in a thick jacket with a whisky bottle sticking out of a pocket, gaping open-mouthed at something he saw in the sky. Santa Claus and his reindeers zooming through the scudding clouds! Bingo! There it was. A basic idea, an itch in the mind, a "feel" of a tingle that might become a story. I snatched the bottle out of his pocket, knocked years and whiskers off his face—and Stubby Pringle was riding back to his bunk at the line cabin.

Something was still missing. The vital ingredient, the signal, the message, the spark of story-life. Santa supplied that. Charley Russell's Santa. While I stared at him there on the cover, he drew in a deep breath, puffed out his cheeks, and shouted his salute to Stubby. I had a story to write.

A short story should resemble a short piece of music—individual, complete within itself, with its own form and tempo and rhythm and tune. This one became an experiment in individuality all around.

Third-person approach this time—but not the usual impersonal omniscient narration. Someone telling it, unknown, unidentified, skeptical but sympathetic, really myself in hiding, telling it so that anyone reading it aloud would be telling it too, one person to others. You might call that a kind of hybrid first-person approach. The narrator does not toss in any "I"'s and "me"'s and say that he was there and saw and heard this and that or explain how he knows what happened; but his presence as the narrator is always apparent and he talks directly to his listeners and even to Stubby and offers comments, particularly at the finish. And he does not merely tell the tale. At times he almost chants it in choppy staccato style. At others he almost sings it, especially the recurrent mannered alliterative sentence forms and refrains. Without being fully conscious of this, I was probably trying to concoct a story that needs the human voice for its full effect.

Thinking about it now, I suddenly realize that those are the tricks, the mannerisms, of many ballads. Of folk-songs. I was simply adapting them to a prose story. And again, I suddenly recall that Rudyard Kipling did the same thing with positive genius in his *"Just So Stories."*

There are many stylistic tricks tucked away in "Stubby" for anyone who thinks it worth the nuisance of hunting for them. The one which sticks out farthest and pricks the critics the most is the omission of articles. I played around with that and liked it—in certain places, particularly the semi-chant sections. Then I found myself putting the articles back in other places—where it "felt" right to smooth out into longer flowing clauses and sentences. I followed no real formula or rule, simply my own feeling for the sentences as I shaped them within the form of the story as a whole. Perhaps I was not simply having fun; perhaps I was trying to disguise or overcome with stylistic tricks the fact that the material itself drips sentiment. Deadly stuff, sentiment, which has to be handled very carefully. Especially nowadays.

It took several weeks of fiddling with the basic idea in my mind and a first page in my typewriter before everything, plot and shape and style and tempo, even tune, began to feel right. Then I galloped along like the cat-hipped roan, enjoying myself, and wrote the entire story in two or three days just under the wire for the *Boys' Life* deadline. The following year my book publishers gave it more permanent status in a neat little volume for the annual Christmas trade.

"Stubby" is, of course, a hodge-podge of the literal and the nonliteral. At times it is humdrum, realistic, down-to-actual-life. At others it takes off into what seems to be fantasy, exaggeration, bigger-than-life description—which is what can give the unwary the notion it is meant to be a tall tale. Was that done deliberately as build-up preparation for the unrealistic visionary experience Stubby has while plodding back up the mountain? Perhaps it does help make what happens to him a bit more believable. But for me in the writing, that frequent slipping into tall-tale terms was simply part of the fun, of the experiment, my way of presenting how Stubby felt at each stage of the story—his inner experience at each stage.

When Stubby starts out primed for the dance, his hat, to him, *is* brushing stars in the sky. When he is soaring down the mountain, to himself he *is* ten feet tall and his horse *is* gigantic, iron-boned and dynamite-fueled. When he is doing this and that at the homestead shack, responding to the decency deep in him and using the few skills won out of his own hard life, he *is* an expert born to do such things. When he is plodding back to the cabin he has dwindled even to himself into what on the literal prosaic level he has been all along, just another patched-clothes poorly-paid cowhand on a scrubby cat-hipped cowpony. But when he has seen and heard the message out of the sky, really out of his own subconscious triggered by simple literal things about him, he has caught again the upsurge of strong decent life within him. He would never put this in any such terms, but he has wrung some meaning for his own meagre existence out of an evening of helping others towards a few smiles and a bit of joy of living. Once again he *is* ten feet tall, needing and having a horse gigantic, with wings, more than a match for the night's work.

Myths. Critics like to talk about the use of myths and legends in fiction. Quite the thing nowadays. "Stubby" uses the Santa Claus myth for the one simple precise purpose of making its point, underlining whatever of significance it has as a story. Part of the experiment was to see if I could use old Santa without identifying him by name—keep him an obvious open "secret" shared by me and my readers. After all, he is not really in the story, which has nothing mythical about it. He is there only in the mind of Stubby, a symbol for what Stubby glimpses in the snow mist—glimpsed in the form in which Stubby would visualize it.

This story too aims all along at the final paragraph. Stubby really *is* wiser than most of us. What he knows and always will know—that is, what he has grasped and what will always be with him and what to him took the form of old Santa is what Santa symbolizes, the spirit of Christmas, of friendship and giving and sharing, and not only for once a year at Christmastime but through all the days of the years.

Some of this somewhat high-faluting thinking was actually in my own mind when I wrote "Stubby." Vaguely. In the background. In the "feel" of the story. Most of the time I was simply enjoying myself writing a rather cockeyed kind of tale which had taken on its own peculiar shape and was being done to fulfill an assignment I had accepted. "Jacob" is a better story, firmer, better done, stronger in its material and less dependent on tricks in the telling. But "Stubby" was more fun in the writing—and may be for some in the reading.

It seems to me, too, that "Stubby" is one story which, once it has been read and "heard" and grasped as a whole by the reader, almost demands discussion of the devices used. They are so much and so obviously a part of it and the writer, myself, frankly admits they were consciously and deliberately added to the basic story idea. It may be that "Stubby" is an example of a story in which over-attention to techniques has over-burdened the telling of the tale. Do those deliberate devices really contribute to the overall effect? Are they needed to achieve it? Do they, as the writer thought and hoped in the writing, make what is essentially just another maudlin sentimental version of the Christmas cliché a bit more interesting, perhaps more memorable, more effective?

Is Stubby himself, in spite of or perhaps because of the mannered way in which he is presented, a believable human being? Did he tell Old Jake a simple truth? "Why, sure, I had me a right good time." And if he did, does that have any meaning for the rest of us?

BIOGRAPHICAL NOTE

Photo: Eli Wallach

Roald Dahl was born in Wales in 1916 and grew up there and in Kent. His first published writing, an account of his experiences as a fighter pilot in the Royal Air Force, was published in the *Saturday Evening Post.* His first book of stories dealt largely with flying, too. But it is the kind of story appearing in two later collections that Dahl is best known for. These are macabre, grisly, and often funny stories, beautifully contrived and richly suspenseful. Many stories deal with conflicts between the sexes; each sex wins its victories.

Dahl and his wife, actress Patricia Neal, now live in Buckinghamshire. There Dahl, the father of four, writes and enjoys such hobbies as buying and selling paintings, growing roses, and collecting eighteenth-century furniture. He likes to gamble, too, and specializes in horseraces. His knowledge of wines figures prominently in his most widely anthologized story, "Taste," which begins on p. 97. Other stories frequently anthologized include "The Great Automatic Grammatisator," "Parson's Pleasure," and "Lamb to the Slaughter."

His books include:

Over to You	Reynal,	1946
Someone Like You	Knopf,	1953
Kiss Kiss	Knopf,	1960
James and the Giant Peach	Knopf,	1961
Charlie and the Chocolate Factory	Knopf,	1964
Magic Finger	Harper & Row,	1966

The *Atlantic Monthly, The New Yorker,* and *Playboy* are among the magazines carrying his stories. His Knopf collections have been frequently mined for anthologies, TV scripts, and movie scenarios.

In his response to my letter inviting him to say some things about teaching short stories, Dahl wrote, "I would consider doing what you asked provided I could say what I wished." In the pages following, he has.

PART THREE

Plot and Circumstance

Roald Dahl

I don't know what it is like now, but in 1923, when I started going to boarding school in England at the age of seven, the teaching of English took precedence over all other subjects in the curriculum. The ability to write clear short sentences which said precisely what one meant them to say was unquestionably the number one requirement. Our whole education was subtly but relentlessly directed toward this end. Everything we wrote was examined and checked and corrected with the utmost care. We were not even permitted to mail letters home to our mothers without the headmaster reading them first; and nine times out of ten he would hand them back to us, not so often for grammatical correction as for general improvement. "That is a ridiculously muddled paragraph," he would say. "Try it again. Explain it more simply. Make your mother see it and feel it as though she were there with you at the time. Mention the tiny little things."

At the age of nine, we were writing three essays a week (compositions I think they are called now), and one out of the three had always to be a made-up story with a plot. I still have an exercise book filled with the essays of that time, and what is remarkable about them is not the essays themselves but the meticulous care with which the teacher (Mr. Victor Corrado) had corrected them. "I think," he wrote once (in the margin) to my nine-year-old self, "that *troubled* might be a better adjective to use here than *glum*. *Troubled face* is preferable to *glum face*. Or you might use *brooding* or *baleful* or *desolate*. *Ruthful* is rare but acceptable. There are many others. Choose the best one, but do so with very great care, for each has a slightly different meaning."

At the age of ten, while the teaching of writing continued as intensely as ever, the teaching of literature was added to the syllabus, and we embarked upon a two-year course with a lady whom I shall never forget, called Mrs. O'Connor (no relation to Frank). Mrs. O'Connor had huge yellow teeth and a radiant enthusiasm for the classics. To each of us, on the first day of term, she handed a long list of dates and names. This was her "Chronological Table," and it contained, according to her, most of the great landmarks in the history of literature—one hundred of them in all. She then told us that we must know the whole of this list by heart (dodging about as well as in order) by the end of that first term, learning it out of school hours. Tradition decreed that anyone who did not know it by then would be sent to the headmaster (Mr. A. J. H. Francis) to be whacked, and when Mr. Francis whacked you, he used a thin whippy yellow cane, and the deep blue corrugated lines which it left upon your bottom throbbed for a week afterwards as you lay in bed at night after the lights were put out.

The fear of a whacking seared Mrs. O'Connor's Chronological Table so deeply into my brain that now, thirty-seven years later, I can still remember bits of it here and there without even stopping to think. It started with 597 St. Augustine lands in Thanet. Then, 731 Bede's Ecclesiastical History. Some of the others that come immediately to the surface are 1485 Malory's Morte d'Arthur, 1477 Caxton sets up his printing press in England, 1478 Chaucer's Canterbury Tales, 1605 Cervantes' Don Quixote, 1623 the First Folio of Shakespeare, 1633 Milton's L'Allegro and Il Penseroso, 1711 Addison's Spectator, 1755 Johnson's Dictionary, 1776 Gibbon's Decline and Fall, 1776 Adam Smith's Wealth of Nations, 1818 Evelyn's Diary, 1833 Carlyle's Sartor Resartus, 1857 Flaubert's Madame Bovary, 1859 Darwin's Origin of Species, 1869 Tolstoy's War and Peace.

There were, as I said, no less than one hundred of them altogether. It would be an interesting but severe test of literary knowledge for a class of students to be asked to compile a similar list. It would be quite a test for a teacher as well. The list should stop, as Mrs. O'Connor's did, at the end of the nineteenth century.

Over the next two years, while we were ageing from ten to twelve, Mrs. O'Connor went slowly right through her Chronological Table, taking the items one by one and devoting four separate hours to each. She must have been a lady of immense knowledge and wisdom. Her classes were never dull. It was thrilling the way she told us about the lives of these great men, and wonderful it was to hear her reading aloud the best and most significant passages from their works. Even Adam Smith sounded exciting by the time Mrs. O'Connor had gotten through with him. And at the end of it all, when we were twelve years old and beginning to move on to our next and last school, we took with us, thanks to this lady and indeed to all six teachers at that little school, a genuine love of literature.

In the big school, the same process was continued. There were thirty-eight scholarly teachers there, and every one of them (with the exception of the physics and chemistry masters) paid particular attention to the writing and the reading of the English language. I can remember a French teacher (Mr. S. H. Wall)—and don't forget it was *not* his job officially to teach us English—I can remember him finding a split infinitive in somebody's translation of Victor Hugo. He read it out to us aloud, snorting with contempt, and then he said, "Splitting an infinitive is like separating a child from his mother. It is unnatural and offensive. Nobody who is kind and gentle could be persuaded to commit such a crime. And now listen to me. For the next twelve months, holidays included, I will give half-a-crown for every split infinitive that any of you can find in *The Times.*" (*The London Times* newspaper.) Half-a-crown in those days would buy you fifteen good-size bars of chocolate, and it must have been the equivalent in value to about a dollar-fifty today. Thus, by this simple device, Mr. S. H. Wall compelled the twenty-eight greedy little boys in his class not only to read assiduously the best-written newspaper in the world from end to end every day, but also compelled them to be conscious for the rest of their lives of one of the ugliest practices in our language. None of us ever found a split infinitive in *The Times,* but at the same time, I am willing to bet that none of us has ever, since then, split an infinitive either in speech or on paper. I am fairly sure that I never have.

All of us at this last school were taught to admire the short story. From the age of twelve right through to eighteen, short stories were continually being read to us aloud by our teachers, and the secret here, of course, was never to choose a bad one. There were, in those days, plenty of good ones available. For the first twenty-five years of this century, England was the fountainhead of the short story. And what excellent stories most of them were. They had plots. The plots progressed swiftly. The tension or the humour built up and up and up. Then came an explosion. It was wonderful. And we, hearing them read to us in the classrooms, thought they were absolutely super. To our ways of thinking, there was nothing to beat a short story.

Today very few short stories are absolutely super. The beautifully written ones seem always to be those plotless and dreadfully dull mood pieces that we know so well. The badly written ones are often clumsy or vulgar. Now and again a real beauty comes along, but it is a rare event. I would recommend strongly that a teacher should never read mood pieces or semi-plots or unresolved plots to a class of students if he wishes to teach them to like the short story. He should read them something that he knows positively is going to stimulate them, something that will create a bit of a buzz throughout the whole classroom when the last sentence has been spoken.

The reason for the spate of plotless stories nowadays is twofold. Firstly, they are easier to write than the plotty ones, and secondly, the plots themselves are very difficult indeed to come by. Every month they get scarcer and scarcer. Anecdotes are common, but an anecdote is not a plot. My main preoccupation when I am writing a story is a constant unholy terror of boring the reader, and because I myself become very rapidly bored (this is probably a severe failing) by anything that does not possess a good strong plot, I fancy, probably quite wrongly, that other people feel the same way. Take this particular piece that I am writing now. I think it is dreadful. It has no plot or direction. I am certain that it makes dull reading, and because of that, I am constantly having to stop myself from rushing off at a tangent to tell some story that I think would be more interesting. I nearly got going on the subject of my schooldays with Mr. A. J. H. Francis and his whippy yellow cane. That would have been splendid, but not, I'm afraid, to the point.

The point here, I am told, is to try to say something that will help teachers to teach the short story to their pupils. In this I shall fail. Writers do not make good teachers any more than married men make good husbands. Once in a while there is an exception, but as a general rule, professional writers should not try to teach anything to anybody. They should stick to writing. Teaching is an art in itself, and the ability to teach well is a gift that cannot be acquired casually. If, in this brief rambling discourse, I should happen to say anything helpful, I shall be surprised.

Let it be assumed, however, that I am *forced* to stand up before a class and teach the short story. Very well. I shall do my best. But my methods will appear clumsy and amateur to professional teachers, and not especially original, so make allowances, if you please.

I should begin by introducing my pupils to a number of stories that I had selected myself with the utmost care—absolutely first-rate stories that I knew for certain would not bore anybody. These are scarce, but they can be found. I would then read these stories aloud one after the other to my class, giving the minimum time for discussion and no time whatsoever for analysis as I went along. By starting out in this way, I would hope to convince my pupils that the proper short story, the one that is constructed with infinite care and patience by the expert, is a marvellously entertaining thing. They would learn that it was brief, easy to read, easy to understand, intensely exciting, or amusing, or moving, a minor treasure designed not to instruct or uplift the reader but merely to divert him for twenty minutes or so when he happened to be in the mood.

That, you see, is precisely what the short story is—a diversion. You don't settle yourself down comfortably with a short story for an hour or two as you do with a shortish novel. You pick it up casually when you happen to have a few minutes to kill, perhaps at the hairdresser's, or before supper in the evening, or while travelling to work on the bus. *And the good story writer is well aware of this.* He knows that you are going to be in a tricky mood when you start reading. He knows that you will probably be "unsettled" and reluctant to give your undivided attention. And as he begins to write his story, he pictures you in, let us say, the dentist's waiting-room, twelve months hence, and you pick up a magazine and you find his story (now finished and published) and you begin to read it. You read five lines, then suddenly you hear a yell of agony from the next room as the point of the dentist's drill penetrates the root canal of the bicuspid of the patient who is in there before you. You read another few lines. You stop. You glance up, thinking about the injection that the man will soon be putting into your gum, and about the sound of the drill, and whether you will need an inlay instead of just an ordinary filling, and . . . and . . . and . . .

It is in circumstances such as this (in magazines) that the modern short story is most widely read. But even when the reader is lying comfortably in bed with a whole collection of stories propped upon his chest, I believe that he is still basically an unwilling and reluctant customer. By now he has read too many bad stories to trust them any more, too many rambling dissertations and mood pieces and psychological studies. "Okay," he says as he begins to read, "interest me, and hurry up about it. If you don't do it quickly, I shall open a novel." And the real short story writer accepts this challenge. He tells himself that he has only three or four minutes at most in which to take hold of the reader's brain and compel him to listen. It is a tremendously difficult thing to do.

But to get back to my class of pupils. I have now read them some magnificent stories. They loved them all. They are, I hope, eager for more; and the ones who in the first place were not very keen on the short story as an entertainment have begun to realize they were reading the wrong stuff. At this stage, I would make them play the well-known game of trying to outguess the writer. I would start reading another excellent story to them, but I would stop suddenly when I was about three quarters of the way through. "Write down," I would say, "on half a sheet of paper, a synopsis of how you would end this story. And remember this—that the writer, in choosing to write the story in the first place, is convinced that you cannot outguess him. He is also convinced (or at any rate, he hopes sincerely) that you cannot think up a more interesting final sequence of events than he has done himself. If you can, then the writer has lost."

Finally, I would endeavour, I suppose, to explain to my pupils why this particular form of writing, though so simple to read, is so difficult to execute. And having failed to do this, because I am not a teacher, I should fall back upon telling them a little about my own experience in this field, hoping that they would remain awake to listen.

I have spent the last twenty years of my life writing virtually nothing but short stories—stories for adults and stories for children. I once took six weeks off from stories to write a play, and over the years I have done maybe three short adaptations of my work for television; but apart from those very brief excursions, it has been stories all along the line. I have not even reviewed a book. (I do not anyway approve of one writer criticising another in print. It does no good to either of them. It is a job for professional critics.) And all I have to show for those twenty years of more or less continuous work, morning and afternoon, seven days a week, are thirty-nine little tales, none of which would take you more than twenty-five minutes to read. This means that I have produced not quite two a year.

This absurdly meagre output is due partly to my inability to think up enough plots, but mainly to the ridiculous slowness with which I write. If a thousand superlative plots were spinning around in my head and screaming to be written, I could still only manage to convert two or three of them a year into stories.

Four days ago I finished a new story. It is called "The Visitor." I began it early in September. Today is March 11. I have been working on it continuously in between those two dates, sitting in my little hut in the orchard for three hours each morning and two each afternoon, writing it and rewriting it, trying, as Mr. Victor Corrado taught me at my prep school, to choose the right adjectives, and trying to shorten the sentences and paragraphs, and reducing and condensing and evaporating and crystallizing and cutting the whole thing until I feel that it can be crystallized and cut no more.

Each session begins with a sharpening of pencils. Then I reread not merely the previous day's work but everything I have done up to then, right from the beginning. This means, if you care to work it out, that by the time I am nearing the end of a story, the first part will have been reread and altered and corrected at least one hundred and fifty times.

The very first page of a new story usually takes about two weeks to write, but during those two weeks all sorts of things, I imagine, are being plotted and planned further along the way. Even so, it is an awful struggle, that first page, and a great relief when it is done.

I am sure that this slowness is due to some kind of inadequacy on my part, and I often tell myself that almost *anybody*, if he could bring himself to spend months and months doing nothing else but playing around with one simple little story, could produce the same result. Men in other jobs whom I know, physicists, pathologists, doctors, stockbrokers, shopkeepers, advertisers, farmers, accountants, charladies, bankers, and surgeons, all bustling about like mad from morning till night, regard me (as they do all writers) with a kind of amused tolerance, as they would a child playing with toys in the nursery, and although nobody is ever allowed to interrupt *them* in *their* work (it is far too important), they think nothing of interrupting me in mine. If I produced a story a week and had three volumes published a year, that would be different. I would have something to show for it. But I console myself, on the days of depression, with thoughts of Monsieur Flaubert, reclining upon his sofa, patiently and painstakingly writing and rewriting his *Madame Bovary* for six years straight.

I am suspicious of both facility and speed. Good writing is essentially rewriting. I am positive of this. Thurber used to say it was impossible for a first or even a second draft to be presentable. A long time ago, he told me how his wife once happened to pick up and read the first draft of some story he was doing, and she brought it to him and said, "This is shocking! It's no good at all!" To which he replied, "You wait till you see the final version."

Very few ordinary readers are conscious of the care with which a real short story writer writes his stories, or of the work that goes into them. They are written primarily to be read aloud, which the novel is not. And if they are not read aloud, they should anyway be read slowly. Most reading nowadays is little more than skimming. This I detest. It is impossible to appreciate style or subtlety of language if one reads swiftly. Most people are proud of the fact when they are fast readers, and in the United States much has been made lately of a reading course which will teach the pupil to devour God knows how many thousands of words a minute with his eyes. Speed and more speed! I loathe it all. It is idiotic to read a piece of good writing as fast as one can. If you have before you a dish of foie gras and fresh truffles and if you wish to appreciate it fully, you don't grab your fork and crouch forward and see how quickly you can gulp it down. You take it slowly, savouring each morsel. The same with reading. Reading should be three parts pondering, gloating, dreaming of the thing that is being read. If reading to oneself, one may go at a pace slightly faster than if one were reading aloud, but only *slightly* faster. Newspapers, insurance policies, and all indifferent writing may be read as quickly as possible, but not good writing. I usually take about a week to read a shortish novel. I took two weeks over Elizabeth Bowen's last book. I missed nothing. I savoured every intricate phrase and every carefully woven sentence.

Complete concentration is essential in reading. Where no mental effort is made, no impression is left behind. Though it be purely for enjoyment or diversion, good reading is a consciously creative act. Schopenhauer said that it is thinking with other people's brains, and he put it well.

What else can I tell you? Not very much. I have a notebook for plots. It is the same one I've had for twenty years. If I get the germ of an idea, I scribble it in the notebook, one idea to each page. And there the idea remains, usually for about five years before being used, if it is used at all. But once or twice every year, I leaf through the book, and I pause briefly at every plot note, and I think about it for a few moments, and if I can, I develop it a shade further in my mind. And then at last, perhaps after three years, perhaps after seven, there comes a time when I look at it and I see that it is ripe for writing, and I take it out of the book, and start away. A few of the plot notes that have been written and ticked off read as follows:

Try debunking a wine snob. Have him bet? Have him cheat? (This note became "Taste." [See p. 97.])

Do a murder with a leg of lamb from the deep-freeze. Police could eat lamb later. (This became "Lamb to the Slaughter.")

Could an animal (a cat?) be a celebrated dead composer reincarnated? (This became "Edward the Conqueror.")

Antique dealers will go any lengths to get stuff cheap. Have one of them bargain for a magnificent piece, saying he only wants the legs. The rest is firewood. So the owner cuts it up. (This became "Parson's Pleasure.")

A woman leaves her husband stuck in the elevator in their empty house. Send woman and servants away to get house empty. (This became "The Way up to Heaven.")

Have a beekeeper feed his baby with royal jelly to make him grow. (This became "Royal Jelly.")

And so on and so forth—the germs of plots, germs which must be given time to mature and ripen if they are to be any good at all.

One last thing. Every story that has an element of horror in it must contain, in equal proportions, an element of humour. This is essential. A horror story without humour is vulgar and offensive, and a cultivated reader will always reject it out of hand.

The Landlady

Roald Dahl

Billy Weaver had travelled down from London on the slow afternoon train, with a change at Swindon on the way, and by the time he got to Bath it was about nine o'clock in the evening and the moon was coming up out of a clear starry sky over the houses opposite the station entrance. But the air was deadly cold and the wind was like a flat blade of ice on his cheeks.

"Excuse me," he said, "but is there a fairly cheap hotel not too far away from here?"

"Try The Bell and Dragon," the porter answered, pointing down the road. "They might take you in. It's about a quarter of a mile along on the other side."

Billy thanked him and picked up his suitcase and set out to walk the quarter-mile to The Bell and Dragon. He had never been to Bath before. He didn't know anyone who lived there. But Mr. Greenslade at the Head Office in London had told him it was a splendid city. "Find your own lodgings," he had said, "and then go along and report to the Branch Manager as soon as you've got yourself settled."

Billy was seventeen years old. He was wearing a new navy-blue overcoat, a new brown trilby hat, and a new brown suit, and he was feeling fine. He walked briskly down the street. He was trying to do everything briskly these days. Briskness, he had decided, was *the* one common characteristic of all successful businessmen. The big shots up at Head Office were absolutely fantastically brisk all the time. They were amazing.

There were no shops on this wide street that he was walking along, only a line of tall houses on each side, all of them identical. They had porches and pillars and four or five steps going up to their front doors, and it was obvious that once upon a time they had been very swanky residences. But now, even in the darkness, he could see that the paint was peeling from the woodwork on their doors and windows, and that the handsome white facades were cracked and blotchy from neglect.

Suddenly, in a downstairs window that was brilliantly illuminated by a street-lamp not six yards away, Billy caught sight of a printed notice propped up against the glass in one of the upper panes. It said BED AND BREAKFAST. There was a vase of yellow chrysanthemums, tall and beautiful, standing just underneath the notice.

He stopped walking. He moved a bit closer. Green curtains (some sort of velvety material) were hanging down on either side of the window. The chrysanthemums looked wonderful beside them. He went right up and peered through the glass into the room, and the first thing he saw was a bright fire burning in the hearth. On the carpet in front of the fire, a pretty little dachshund was curled up asleep with its nose tucked into its belly. The room itself, so far as he could see in the half-darkness, was filled with pleasant furniture. There was a baby-grand piano and big sofa and several plump armchairs; and in one corner he spotted a large parrot in a cage. Animals were usually a good sign in a place like this, Billy told himself; and all in all, it looked to him as though it would be a pretty decent house to stay in. Certainly it would be more comfortable than The Bell and Dragon.

On the other hand, a pub would be more congenial than a boarding-house. There would be beer and darts in the evenings, and lots of people to talk to, and it would probably be a good bit cheaper, too. He had stayed a couple of nights in a pub once before and he had liked it. He had never stayed in any boarding-houses, and, to be perfectly honest, he was a tiny bit frightened of them. The name itself conjured up images of watery cabbage, rapacious landladies, and a powerful smell of kippers in the living-room.

After dithering about like this in the cold for two or three minutes, Billy decided that he would walk on and take a look at The Bell and Dragon before making up his mind. He turned to go.

And now a queer thing happened to him. He was in the act of stepping back and turning away from the window when all at once his eye was caught and held in the most peculiar manner by the small notice that was there. BED AND BREAKFAST, it said. BED AND BREAKFAST, BED AND BREAKFAST, BED AND BREAKFAST. Each word was like a large black eye staring at him through the glass, holding him, compelling him, forcing him to stay where he was and not to walk away from that house, and the next thing he knew, he was actually moving across from the window to the front door of the house, climbing the steps that led up to it, and reaching for the bell.

He pressed the bell. Far away in a back room he heard it ringing, and then *at once*—it must have been at once because he hadn't even had time to take his finger from the bell-button—the door swung open and a woman was standing there.

Normally you ring the bell and you have at least a half-minute's wait before the door opens. But this dame was like a jack-in-the-box. He pressed the bell—and out she popped! It made him jump.

She was about forty-five or fifty years old, and the moment she saw him, she gave him a warm welcoming smile.

"*Please* come in," she said pleasantly. She stepped aside, holding the door wide open, and Billy found himself automatically starting forward. The compulsion or, more accurately, the desire to follow after her into that house was extraordinarily strong.

"I saw the notice in the window," he said, holding himself back.

"Yes, I know."

"I was wondering about a room."

"It's *all* ready for you, my dear," she said. She had a round pink face and very gentle blue eyes.

"I was on my way to The Bell and Dragon," Billy told her. "But the notice in your window just happened to catch my eye."

"My dear boy," she said, "why don't you come in out of the cold?"

"How much do you charge?"

"Five and sixpence a night, including breakfast."

It was fantastically cheap. It was less than half of what he had been willing to pay.

"If that is too much," she added, "then perhaps I can reduce it just a tiny bit. Do you desire an egg for breakfast? Eggs are expensive at the moment. It would be sixpence less without the egg."

"Five and sixpence is fine," he answered. "I should like very much to stay here."

"I knew you would. Do come in."

She seemed terribly nice. She looked exactly like the mother of one's best school-friend welcoming one into the house to stay for the Christmas holidays. Billy took off his hat, and stepped over the threshold.

"Just hang it there," she said, "and let me help you with your coat."

There were no other hats or coats in the hall. There were no umbrellas, no walking-sticks—nothing.

"We have it *all* to ourselves," she said, smiling at him over her shoulder as she led the way upstairs. "You see, it isn't very often I have the pleasure of taking a visitor into my little nest."

The old girl is slightly dotty, Billy told himself. But at five and sixpence a night, who gives a damn about that? "I should've thought you'd be simply swamped with applicants," he said politely.

"Oh, I am, my dear, I am, of course I am. But the trouble is that I'm inclined to be just a teeny weeny bit choosy and particular—if you see what I mean."

"Ah, yes."

"But I'm always ready. Everything is always ready day and night in this house just on the off-chance that an acceptable young gentleman will come along. And it is such a pleasure, my dear, such a very great pleasure when now and again I open the door and I see someone standing there who is just *exactly* right." She was halfway up the stairs, and she paused with one hand on the stair-rail, turning her head and smiling down at him with pale lips. "Like you," she added, and her blue eyes travelled slowly all the way down the length of Billy's body, to his feet, and then up again.

On the second-floor landing she said to him, "This floor is mine."

They climbed up another flight. "And this one is *all* yours," she said. "Here's your room. I do hope you'll like it." She took him into a small but charming front bedroom, switching on the light as she went in.

"The morning sun comes right in the window, Mr. Perkins. It *is* Mr. Perkins, isn't it?"

"No," he said. "It's Weaver."

"Mr. Weaver. How nice. I've put a water-bottle between the sheets to air them out, Mr. Weaver. It's such a comfort to have a hot water-bottle in a strange bed with clean sheets, don't you agree? And you may light the gas fire at any time if you feel chilly."

"Thank you," Billy said. "Thank you ever so much." He noticed that the bedspread had been taken off the bed, and that the bedclothes had been neatly turned back on one side, all ready for someone to get in.

"I'm so glad you appeared," she said, looking earnestly into his face. "I was beginning to get worried."

"That's all right," Billy answered brightly. "You mustn't worry about me." He put his suitcase on the chair and started to open it.

"And what about supper, my dear? Did you manage to get anything to eat before you came here?"

"I'm not a bit hungry, thank you," he said. "I think I'll just go to bed as soon as possible because tomorrow I've got to get up rather early and report to the office."

"Very well, then. I'll leave you now so that you can unpack. But before you go to bed, would you be kind enough to pop into the sitting-room on the ground floor and sign the book? Everyone has to do that because its the law of the land, and we don't want to go breaking any laws at *this* stage in the proceedings, do we?" She gave him a little wave of the hand and went quickly out of the room and closed the door.

Now, the fact that his landlady appeared to be slightly off her rocker didn't worry Billy in the least. After all, she not only was harmless—there was no question about that—but she was also quite obviously a kind and generous soul. He guessed that she had probably lost a son in the war, or something like that, and had never gotten over it.

So a few minutes later, after unpacking his suitcase and washing his hands, he trotted downstairs to the ground floor and entered the living-room. His landlady wasn't there, but the fire was glowing in the hearth, and the little dachshund was still sleeping soundly in front of it. The room was wonderfully warm and cosy. I'm a lucky fellow, he thought, rubbing his hands. This is a bit of all right.

He found the guest-book lying open on the piano, so he took out his pen and wrote down his name and address. There were only two other entries above his on the page, and, as one always does with guest-books, he started to read them. One was a Christopher Mulholland from Cardiff. The other was Gregory W. Temple from Bristol.

That's funny, he thought suddenly. Christopher Mulholland. It rings a bell.

Now where on earth had he heard that rather unusual name before?

Was it a boy at school? No. Was it one of his sister's numerous young men, perhaps, or a friend of his father's? No, no, it wasn't any of those. He glanced down again at the book.

Christopher Mulholland   *231 Cathedral Road, Cardiff*

Gregory W. Temple   *27 Sycamore Drive, Bristol*

As a matter of fact, now he came to think of it, he wasn't at all sure that the second name didn't have almost as much of a familiar ring about it as the first.

"Gregory Temple?" he said aloud, searching his memory. "Christopher Mulholland? . . ."

"Such charming boys," a voice behind him answered, and he turned and saw his landlady sailing into the room with a large silver tea-tray in her hands. She was holding it well out in front of her, and rather high up, as though the tray were a pair of reins on a frisky horse.

"They sound somehow familiar," he said.

"They do? How interesting."

"I'm almost positive I've heard those names before somewhere. Isn't that odd? Maybe it was in the newspapers. They weren't famous in any way, were they? I mean famous cricketers or footballers or something like that?"

"Famous," she said, setting the tea-tray down on the low table in front of the sofa. "Oh no, I don't think they were famous. But they were incredibly handsome, both of them, I can promise you that. They were tall and young and handsome, my dear, just exactly like you."

Once more, Billy glanced down at the book. "Look here," he said, noticing the dates. "This last entry is over two years old."

"It is?"

"Yes, indeed. And Christopher Mulholland's is nearly a year before that—more than *three years* ago."

"Dear me," she said, shaking her head and heaving a dainty little sigh. "I would never have thought it. How time does fly away from us all, doesn't it, Mr. Wilkins?"

"It's Weaver," Billy said. "W-e-a-v-e-r."

"Oh, of course it is!" she cried, sitting down on the sofa. "How silly of me. I do apologize. In one ear and out the other, that's me, Mr. Weaver."

"You know something?" Billy said. "Something that's really quite extraordinary about all this?"

"No, dear, I don't."

"Well, you see, both of these names—Mulholland and Temple—I not only seem to remember each one of them separately, so to speak, but somehow or other, in some peculiar way, they both appear to be sort of connected together as well. As though they were both famous for the same sort of thing, if you see what I mean—like . . . well . . . like Dempsey and Tunney, for example, or Churchill and Roosevelt."

"How amusing," she said. "But come over here now, dear, and sit down beside me on the sofa and I'll give you a nice cup of tea and a ginger biscuit before you go to bed."

"You really shouldn't bother," Billy said. "I didn't mean you to do anything like that." He stood by the piano, watching her as she fussed about with the cups and saucers. He noticed that she had small, white, quickly moving hands, and red finger-nails.

"I'm almost positive it was in the newspapers I saw them," Billy said. "I'll think of it in a second. I'm sure I will."

There is nothing more tantalizing than a thing like this that lingers just outside the borders of one's memory. He hated to give up.

"Now wait a minute," he said. "Wait just a minute. Mulholland . . . Christopher Mulholland . . . wasn't *that* the name of the Eton schoolboy who was on a walking-tour through the West Country, and then all of a sudden . . ."

"Milk?" she said. "And sugar?"

"Yes, please. And then all of a sudden . . ."

"Eton schoolboy?" she said. "Oh no, my dear, that can't possibly be right because *my* Mr. Mulholland was certainly not an Eton schoolboy when he came to me. He was a Cambridge undergraduate. Come over here now and sit next to me and warm yourself in front of this lovely fire. Come on. Your tea's all ready for you." She patted the empty place beside her on the sofa, and she sat there smiling at Billy and waiting for him to come over.

He crossed the room slowly, and sat down on the edge of the sofa. She placed his teacup on the table in front of him.

"*There* we are," she said. "How nice and cosy this is, isn't it?"

Billy started sipping his tea. She did the same. For half a minute or so, neither of them spoke. But Billy knew that she was looking at him. Her body was half turned toward him, and he could feel her eyes resting on his face, watching him over the rim of her teacup. Now and again, he caught a whiff of a peculiar smell that seemed to emanate directly from her person. It was not in the least unpleasant, and it reminded him—well, he wasn't quite sure what it reminded him of. Pickled walnuts? New leather? Or was it the corridors of a hospital?

At length, she said, "Mr. Mulholland was a great one for his tea. Never in my life have I seen anyone drink as much tea as dear, sweet Mr. Mulholland."

"I suppose he left fairly recently," Billy said. He was still puzzling his head about the two names. He was positive now that he had seen them in the newspapers—in the headlines.

"Left?" she said, arching her brows. "But my dear boy, he never left. He's still here. Mr. Temple is also here. They're on the fourth floor, both of them together."

Billy set his cup down slowly on the table and stared at his landlady.

She smiled back at him, and then she put out one of her white hands and patted him comfortingly on the knee. "How old are you, my dear?" she asked.

"Seventeen."

"Seventeen!" she cried. "Oh, it's the perfect age! Mr. Mulholland was also seventeen. But I think he was a trifle shorter than you are; in fact I'm sure he was, and his teeth weren't *quite* so white. You have the most beautiful teeth, Mr. Weaver, did you know that?"

"They're not as good as they look," Billy said. "They've got simply masses of fillings in them at the back."

"Mr. Temple, of course, was a little older," she said, ignoring his remark. "He was actually twenty-eight. And yet I never would have guessed it if he hadn't told me, never in my whole life. There wasn't a *blemish* on his body."

"A what?" Billy said.

"His skin was *just* like a baby's."

There was a pause. Billy picked up his teacup and took another sip of his tea, then he set it down again gently in its saucer. He waited for her to say something else, but she seemed to have lapsed into another of her silences. He sat there staring straight ahead of him into the far corner of the room, biting his lower lip.

"That parrot," he said at last. "You know something? It had me completely fooled when I first saw it through the window. I could have sworn it was alive."

"Alas, no longer."

"It's most terribly clever the way it's been done," he said. "It doesn't look in the least bit dead. Who did it?"

"I did."

"*You* did?"

"Of course," she said. "And have you met my little Basil as well?" She nodded toward the dachshund curled up so comfortably in front of the fire. Billy looked at it. And suddenly he realized that this animal had all the time been just as silent and motionless as the parrot. He put out a hand and touched it gently on the top of its back. The back was hard and cold, and when he pushed the hair to one side with his fingers, he could see the skin underneath, greyish-black and dry and perfectly preserved.

"Good gracious me," he said. "How absolutely fascinating." He turned away from the dog and stared with deep admiration at the little woman beside him on the sofa. "It must be most awfully difficult to do a thing like that."

"Not in the least," she said. "I stuff *all* my little pets myself when they pass away. Will you have another cup of tea?"

"No, thank you," Billy said. The tea tasted faintly of bitter almonds, and he didn't much care for it.

"You did sign the book, didn't you?"

"Oh, yes."

"That's good. Because later on, if I happen to forget what you were called, then I could always come down here and look it up. I still do that almost every day with Mr. Mulholland and Mr. . . . . Mr. . . . ."

"Temple," Billy said. "Gregory Temple. Excuse my asking, but haven't there been *any* other guests here except them in the last two or three years?"

Holding her teacup high in one hand, inclining her head slightly to the left, she looked up at him out of the corners of her eyes and gave him another gentle little smile.

"No, my dear," she said. "Only you."

Roald Dahl comments on "The Landlady"

I have wanted for years to write a successful ghost story, and "The Landlady," in its original form, which was never published, was an abortive attempt at this. I thought I had a sound plot, but I hadn't. A really good ghost story is the most difficult of all stories to bring off. In writing it you must violate the golden rule of story telling, which is, and I feel fairly sure about this, that the story *must* be "possible." Let it be as fantastic as you please, but at the end of it all, when the reader looks up and says to himself, "But that's absurd, it could never happen," another voice within him must answer immediately, "Couldn't it? Are you *quite* sure?"

This, incidentally, is where a lot of science fiction goes wrong. Science fiction, and indeed any kind of fiction, becomes boring when the mind refuses to accept the related events as being possible. I myself get most pleasure of all from attempting to write the kind of story which leads the reader so far out into the realms of absurdity or horror that he finally throws up his hands and cries out, "It's ridiculous! It could never be!" And then, at exactly that point, just when he has begun to feel relieved at the thought that such things could not occur in the world he lives in, he suddenly realizes that, by God, they could!

But in a ghost story, you cannot hope to convince many intelligent readers that ghosts exist. You may come close to it, but coming close to it is not enough. So unless you are either very lucky or very clever, your ghost story will fail. Nearly all of them do. I have read just about every ghost story that has ever been printed, and among them all—there are several thousand—I found no more than thirty or so that were acceptable. Half a dozen were beauties. Try "Harry" by Rosemary Timperley, or "The Doctor" by Mary Fitt.

In the ghost version of "The Landlady," the story started out precisely as it does now, with a young boy coming into a town which he had never visited before. He looks for lodgings, he finds them, and is welcomed in by the landlady. Up to this point, the original story was word for word like the present one. But from then on, in the ghost version, the following sequence of events takes place:

1. The boy spends the night in the boarding-house, unharmed.

2. A few moderately disturbing things occur during the night. These things don't worry the boy very much (he is extremely naïve), but they worry the reader.

3. The next day, the boy goes to work. When he returns to his lodgings in the evening, the lodgings aren't there. The house is derelict, an empty shell.

4. The boy, flabbergasted, asks a passer-by about the house. The passer-by tells him that it hasn't been lived in for thirty years. A woman used to live there then, the passer-by explains, and she used indeed to take in lodgers, but she murdered them all, one after the other, etc. etc.

In this unsatisfactory and not very original form, the story went off to *The New Yorker*. It came back with a note from Roger Angell, the chief fiction editor, saying what a pity it was that the story failed because in his opinion the beginning of it was as nearly perfect as a beginning could be.

I have an immense respect for sound editorial advice. So has any writer but a foolish one. I accepted Roger Angell's word for it that the ghost story was no good. I also took his word for it that the first few pages were excellent; and having done that, I set out to see if I couldn't find an entirely new plot to fit in with the old beginning.

Now this is dangerous practice, and I recommend it to nobody. I was exceedingly lucky to happen upon a brand new continuation which turned out to be acceptable.

How to teach this story to a class is something I would not know. That is why I've been rambling about a bit and evading the point. But once again, if I were *forced* to do so (as I am now because in a light-headed moment I made a promise that I would) then, having first read the thing aloud to my class, I would speak the following nonsense:

Were any of you bored? Six of you only. That's very good. Tell me why you were bored, Mildred. Tell me what you thought the story was about. What? Ah, I see. You thought it was about a lady taxidermist who stuffed her parrot when it died, so that she could always have it with her. Did she stuff any other animals? Her dog, you say. Yes, you are quite right. But nothing else? No. I see.

I can understand why you thought it was boring, but now I

must tell you that this is actually a story about a landlady who doesn't only stuff her dogs and parrots when they pass away, but she stuffs her lodgers as well. She kills them and then stuffs them. And if the story has any merit, that merit lies chiefly in the fact that the imaginative reader, after he has finished it, is compelled to picture to himself a number of curious unspoken possibilities.

What are they?

The landlady seems to like only handsome young men. Why?

Does she turn away hundreds of applicants throughout the year, choosing only the few that take her fancy? It looks like it. If the "To let" sign is always in the window, she must receive callers almost every day.

She is very discriminating in her choices. She seems to insist upon them having smooth skin and white teeth. What can this mean?

What does she *do* with these young men after they have been killed and stuffed? Does she talk to them? Does she dress them up and brush their hair and sit them down with her at table for lunch?

Or does she leave them simply standing about in the room upstairs?

If so, are they naked or clothed?

Does sex enter into it in some peculiar way? It rather looks as though it does.

Each of these unanswered questions can lead the thoughtful reader along an interesting avenue of speculation. The implications are legion. The fit reader will have paused at the end of the story to consider each one of them.

Another point. Is the story possible?

It is. If a good taxidermist can stuff and mount a giraffe or a polar bear (see the Natural History Museum), he or she can certainly do the same to a man.

Would she be caught by the police?

Very unlikely. People who respond to a "Room to let" sign in a house window do it on the spur of the moment, as did our hero, and nobody in the world would know where to look for them when they disappeared. The story is very possible indeed, and we can only hope that it doesn't give anyone ideas.

It is also a story of clues. From a point quite early on, little clues or hints are continually being given to the reader that something queer is going on. It is essential that he read the story carefully enough to pick these up. The clues are gentle at first, but they become more and more pointed as the story nears its conclusion. They are:

"It's *all* ready for you, my dear" (p. 89) . . . This is not normal speech.

There were no other hats or coats in the hall, no walking sticks—nothing (p. 89).

. . . and her eyes travelled all the way down the length of Billy's body, to his feet, and then up again (p. 90).

"I'm so glad you appeared," she said, looking earnestly into his face. "I was beginning to get worried" (p. 90).

". . . we don't want to go breaking any laws at *this* stage of the proceedings, do we?" (p. 90).

There are many more, but you can find them as well as I can.

And, of course, nobody should miss, at p. 93, "The tea tasted faintly of bitter almonds, and he didn't much care for it." That, as everybody should know from experience, is how potassium cyanide tastes in a lethal dose.

Taste

Roald Dahl

There were six of us to dinner that night at Mike Schofield's house in London: Mike and his wife and daughter, my wife and I, and a man called Richard Pratt.

Richard Pratt was a famous gourmet. He was president of a small society known as the Epicures, and each month he circulated privately to its members a pamphlet on food and wines. He organized dinners where sumptuous dishes and rare wines were served. He refused to smoke for fear of harming his palate, and when discussing a wine, he had a curious, rather droll habit of referring to it as though it were a living being. "A prudent wine," he would say, "rather diffident and evasive, but quite prudent." Or, "a good-humored wine, benevolent and cheerful—slightly obscene, perhaps, but nonetheless good-humored."

I had been to dinner at Mike's twice before when Richard Pratt was there, and on each occasion Mike and his wife had gone out of their way to produce a special meal for the famous gourmet. And this one, clearly, was to be no exception. The moment we entered the dining room, I could see that the table was laid for a feast. The tall candles, the yellow roses, the quantity of shining silver, the three wineglasses to each person, and above all, the faint scent of roasting meat from the kitchen brought the first warm oozings of saliva to my mouth.

As we sat down, I remembered that on both Richard Pratt's previous visits Mike had played a little betting game with him over the claret, challenging him to name its breed and its vintage. Pratt had replied that that should not be too difficult provided it was one of the great years. Mike had then bet him a case of the wine in question that he could not do it. Pratt had accepted, and had won both times. Tonight I felt sure that the little game would be played over again, for Mike was quite willing to lose the bet in order to prove that his wine was good enough to be recognized, and Pratt, for his part, seemed to take a grave, restrained pleasure in displaying his knowledge.

The meal began with a plate of whitebait, fried very crisp in butter, and to go with it there was a Moselle. Mike got up and poured the wine himself, and when he sat down again, I could see that he was watching Richard Pratt. He had set the bottle in front of me so that I could read the label. It said "Geierslay Ohligsberg, 1945." He leaned over and whispered to me that Geierslay was a tiny village in the Moselle, almost unknown outside Germany. He said that this wine we were drinking was something unusual, that the output of the vineyard was so small that it was almost impossible for a stranger to get any of it. He had visited Geierslay personally the previous summer in order to obtain the few dozen bottles that they had finally allowed him to have.

"I doubt anyone else in the country has any of it at the moment," he said. I saw him glance again at Richard Pratt. "Great thing about Moselle," he continued, raising his voice, "it's the perfect wine to be served before a claret. A lot of people serve a Rhine wine instead, but that's because they don't know any better. A Rhine wine will kill a delicate claret, you know that? It's barbaric to serve a Rhine before a claret. But a Moselle—ah!—a Moselle is exactly right."

Mike Schofield was an amiable, middle-aged man. But he was a stockbroker. To be precise, he was a jobber in the stock market, and like a number of his kind, he seemed to be somewhat embarrassed, almost ashamed to find that he had made so much money with so slight a talent. In his heart he knew that he was not really much more than a bookmaker—an unctuous, infinitely respectable, secretly unscrupulous bookmaker—and he knew that his friends knew it, too. So he was seeking now to become a man of culture, to cultivate a literary and aesthetic taste, to collect paintings, music, books, and all the rest of it. His little sermon about Rhine wine and Moselle was a part of this thing, this culture that he sought.

"A charming little wine, don't you think?" he said. He was still watching Richard Pratt. I could see him give a rapid furtive glance down the table each time he dropped his head to take a mouthful of whitebait. I could almost *feel* him waiting for the moment when Pratt would take his first sip, and look up from his glass with a smile of pleasure, of astonishment, perhaps even of wonder, and then there would be a discussion and Mike would tell him about the village of Geierslay.

But Richard Pratt did not taste his wine. He was completely engrossed in conversation with Mike's eighteen-year-old daughter, Louise. He was half turned toward her, smiling at her, telling her, so far as I could gather, some story about a chef in a Paris restaurant. As he spoke, he leaned closer and closer to her, seeming in his eagerness almost to impinge upon her, and the poor girl leaned as far as she could away from him, nodding politely, rather desperately, and looking not at his face but at the topmost button of his dinner jacket.

We finished our fish, and the maid came around removing the plates. When she came to Pratt, she saw that he had not yet touched his food, so she hesitated, and Pratt noticed her. He waved her away, broke off his conversation, and quickly began to eat, popping the little crisp brown fish quickly into his mouth with rapid jabbing movements of his fork. Then, when he had finished, he reached for his glass, and in two short swallows he tipped the wine down his throat and turned immediately to resume his conversation with Louise Schofield.

Mike saw it all. I was conscious of him sitting there, very still, containing himself, looking at his guest. His round jovial face seemed to loosen slightly and to sag, but he contained himself and was still and said nothing.

Soon the maid came forward with the second course. This was a large roast of beef. She placed it on the table in front of Mike who stood up and carved it, cutting the slices very thin, laying them gently on the plates for the maid to take around. When he had served everyone, including himself, he put down the carving knife and leaned forward with both hands on the edge of the table.

"Now," he said, speaking to all of us but looking at Richard Pratt. "Now for the claret. I must go and fetch the claret, if you'll excuse me."

"You go and fetch it, Mike?" I said. "Where is it?"

"In my study, with the cork out—breathing."

"Why the study?"

"Acquiring room temperature, of course. It's been there twenty-four hours."

"But why the study?"

"It's the best place in the house. Richard helped me choose it last time he was here."

At the sound of his name, Pratt looked around.

"That's right, isn't it?" Mike said.

"Yes," Pratt answered, nodding gravely. "That's right."

"On top of the green filing cabinet in my study," Mike said. "That's the place we chose. A good draft-free spot in a room with an even temperature. Excuse me now, will you, while I fetch it."

The thought of another wine to play with had restored his humor, and he hurried out the door, to return a minute later more slowly, walking softly, holding in both hands a wine basket in which a dark bottle lay. The label was out of sight, facing downward. "Now!" he cried as he came toward the table. "What about this one, Richard? You'll never name this one!"

Richard Pratt turned slowly and looked up at Mike; then his eyes travelled down to the bottle nestling in its small wicker basket, and he raised his eyebrows, a slight supercilious arching of the brows, and with it a pushing outward of the wet lower lip, suddenly imperious and ugly.

"You'll never get it," Mike said. "Not in a hundred years."

"A claret?" Richard Pratt asked, condescending.

"Of course."

"I assume, then, that it's from one of the smaller vineyards?"

"Maybe it is, Richard. And then again, maybe it isn't."

"But it's a good year? One of the great years?"

"Yes, I guarantee that."

"Then it shouldn't be too difficult," Richard Pratt said, drawling his words, looking exceedingly bored. Except that, to me, there was something strange about his drawling and his boredom: between the shadow of something evil, and in his bearing an intentness that gave me a faint sense of uneasiness as I watched him.

"This one is really difficult," Mike said, "I won't force you to bet on this one."

"Indeed. And why not?" Again the slow arching of the brows, the cool, intent look.

"Because it's difficult."

"That's not very complimentary to me, you know."

"My dear man," Mike said, "I'll bet you with pleasure, if that's what you wish."

"It shouldn't be too hard to name it."

"You mean you want to bet?"

"I'm perfectly willing to bet," Richard Pratt said.

"All right, then, we'll have the usual. A case of the wine itself."

"You don't think I'll be able to name it, do you?"

"As a matter of fact, and with all due respect, I don't," Mike said. He was making some effort to remain polite, but Pratt was not bothering overmuch to conceal his contempt for the whole proceeding. And yet, curiously, his next question seemed to betray a certain interest.

"You like to increase the bet?"

"No, Richard. A case is plenty."

"Would you like to bet fifty cases?"

"That would be silly."

Mike stood very still behind his chair at the head of the table, carefully holding the bottle in its ridiculous wicker basket. There was a trace of whiteness around his nostrils now, and his mouth was shut very tight.

Pratt was lolling back in his chair, looking up at him, the eyebrows raised, the eyes half closed, a little smile touching the corners of his lips. And again I saw, or thought I saw, something distinctly disturbing about the man's face, that shadow of intentness between the eyes and in the eyes themselves, right in their centers where it was black, a small slow spark of shrewdness, hiding.

"So you don't want to increase the bet?"

"As far as I'm concerned, old man, I don't give a damn," Mike said. "I'll bet you anything you like."

The three women and I sat quietly, watching the two men. Mike's wife was becoming annoyed; her mouth had gone sour and I felt that at any moment she was going to interrupt. Our roast beef lay before us on our plates, slowly steaming.

"So you'll bet me anything I like?"

"That's what I told you. I'll bet you anything you damn well please, if you want to make an issue out of it."

"Even ten thousand pounds?"

"Certainly I will, if that's the way you want it." Mike was more confident now. He knew quite well that he could call any sum Pratt cared to mention.

"So you say that I can name the bet?" Pratt asked again.

"That's what I said."

There was a pause while Pratt looked slowly around the table, first at me, then at the three women, each in turn. He appeared to be reminding us that we were witness to the offer.

"Mike!" Mrs. Schofield said. "Mike, why don't we stop this nonsense and eat our food. It's getting cold."

"But it isn't nonsense," Pratt told her evenly. "We're making a little bet."

I noticed the maid standing in the background holding a dish of vegetables, wondering whether to come forward with them or not.

"All right, then," Pratt said. "I'll tell you what I want you to bet."

"Come on, then," Mike said, rather reckless. "I don't give a damn what it is—you're on."

Pratt nodded, and again the little smile moved the corners of his lips, and then, quite slowly, looking at Mike all the time, he said, "I want you to bet me the hand of your daughter in marriage."

Louise Schofield gave a jump. "Hey!" she cried. "No! That's not funny! Look here, Daddy, that's not funny at all."

"No, dear," her mother said. "They're only joking."

"I'm not joking," Richard Pratt said.

"It's ridiculous," Mike said. He was off balance again now.

"You said you'd bet anything I liked."

"I meant money."

"You didn't *say* money."

"That's what I meant."

"Then it's a pity you didn't say it. But anyway, if you wish to go back on your offer, that's quite all right with me."

"It's not a question of going back on my offer, old man. It's a no-bet anyway, because you can't match the stake. You yourself don't happen to have a daughter to put against mine in case you lose. And if you had, I wouldn't want to marry her."

"I'm glad of that, dear," his wife said.

"I'll put up anything you like," Pratt announced. "My house, for example. How about my house?"

"Which one?" Mike asked, joking now.

"The country one."

"Why not the other one as well?"

"All right then, if you wish it. Both my houses."

At that point I saw Mike pause. He took a step forward and placed the bottle in its basket gently down on the table. He moved the saltcellar to one side, then the pepper, and then he picked up his knife, studied the blade thoughtfully for a moment, and put it down again. His daughter, too, had seen him pause.

"Now, Daddy!" she cried. "Don't be *absurd!* It's *too* silly for words. I refuse to be betted on like this."

"Quite right, dear," her mother said. "Stop it at once, Mike, and sit down and eat your food."

Mike ignored her. He looked over at his daughter and he smiled, a slow, fatherly, protective smile. But in his eyes, suddenly, there glimmered a little triumph. "You know," he said, smiling as he spoke. "You know, Louise, we ought to think about this a bit."

"Now, stop it, Daddy! I refuse even to listen to you! Why, I've never heard anything so ridiculous in my life!"

"No, seriously, my dear. Just wait a moment and hear what I have to say."

"But I don't *want* to hear it."

"Louise! Please! It's like this. Richard, here, has offered us a serious bet. He is the one who wants to make it, not I. And if he loses, he will have to hand over a considerable amount of property. Now, wait a minute, my dear, don't interrupt. The point is this. *He cannot possibly win.*"

"He seems to think he can."

"Now listen to me, because I know what I'm talking about. The expert, when tasting a claret—so long as it is not of the famous great wines like Lafite or Latour—can only get a certain way toward naming the vineyard. He can, of course, tell you the Bordeaux district from which the wine comes, whether it is from St. Emilion, Pomerol, Graves, or Médoc. But then each district has several communes, little counties, and each county has many, many small vineyards. It is impossible for a man to differentiate between them all by taste and smell alone. I don't mind telling you that this one I've got here is a wine from a small vineyard that is surrounded by many other small vineyards, and he'll never get it. It's impossible."

"You can't be sure of that," his daughter said.

"I'm telling you I can. Though I say it myself, I understand quite a bit about this wine business, you know. And anyway, heavens alive, girl, I'm your father and you don't think I'd let you in for—for something you didn't want, do you? I'm trying to make you some money."

"Mike!" his wife said sharply. "Stop it now, Mike, please!"

Again he ignored her. "If you will take this bet," he said to his daughter, "in ten minutes you will be the owner of two large houses."

"But I don't want two large houses, Daddy."

"Then sell them. Sell them back to him on the spot. I'll arrange all that for you. And then, just think of it, my dear, you'll be rich! You'll be independent for the rest of your life!"

"Oh, Daddy, I don't like it. I think it's silly."

"So do I," the mother said. She jerked her head briskly up and down as she spoke, like a hen. "You ought to be ashamed of yourself, Michael, ever suggesting such a thing! Your own daughter, too!"

Mike didn't even look at her. "Take it!" he said eagerly, staring hard at the girl. "Take it, quick! I'll guarantee you won't lose."

"But I don't like it, Daddy."

"Come on, girl. Take it!"

Mike was pushing her hard. He was leaning toward her, fixing her with two hard bright eyes, and it was not easy for the daughter to resist him.

"But what if I lose?"

"I keep telling you, you can't lose. I'll guarantee it."

"Oh, Daddy, must I?"

"I'm making you a fortune. So come on now. What do you say, Louise? All right?"

For the last time, she hesitated. Then she gave a helpless little shrug of the shoulders and said, "Oh, all right, then. Just so long as you swear there's no danger of losing."

"Good!" Mike cried. "That's fine! Then it's a bet!"

"Yes," Richard Pratt said, looking at the girl. "It's a bet."

Immediately, Mike picked up the wine, tipped the first thimbleful into his own glass, then skipped excitedly around the table filling up the others. Now everyone was watching Richard Pratt, watching his face as he reached slowly for his glass with his right hand and lifted it to his nose. The man was about fifty years old and he did not have a pleasant face. Somehow, it was all mouth—mouth and lips—the full, wet lips of the professional gourmet, the lower lip hanging downward in the center, a pendulous, permanently open taster's lip, shaped open to receive the rim of a glass or a morsel of food. "Like a keyhole," I thought, watching it; "his mouth is like a large wet keyhole."

Slowly he lifted the glass to his nose. The point of the nose entered the glass and moved over the surface of the wine, delicately sniffing. He swirled the wine gently around in the glass to receive the bouquet. His concentration was intense. He had closed his eyes, and now the whole top half of his body, the head and neck and chest, seemed to become a kind of huge sensitive smelling machine, receiving, filtering, analyzing the message from the sniffing nose.

Mike, I noticed, was lounging in his chair, apparently unconcerned, but he was watching every move. Mrs. Schofield, the wife, sat prim and upright at the other end of the table, looking straight ahead, her face tight with disapproval. The daughter, Louise, had shifted her chair away a little, and sidewise, facing the gourmet, and she, like her father, was watching closely.

For at least a minute, the smelling process continued; then, without opening his eyes or moving his head, Pratt lowered the glass to his mouth and tipped in almost half the contents. He paused, his mouth full of wine, getting the first taste; then he permitted some of it to trickle down his throat and I saw his Adam's apple move as it passed by. But most of it he retained in his mouth. And now, without swallowing again, he drew in through his lips a thin breath of air which mingled with the fumes of the wine in the mouth and passed on down into his lungs. He held the breath, blew it out through his nose, and finally began to roll the wine around under the tongue, and chewed it, actually chewed it with his teeth as though it were bread.

It was a solemn, impressive performance, and I must say he did it well.

"Um," he said, putting down the glass, running a pink tongue over his lips. "Um—yes. A very interesting little wine—gentle and gracious, almost feminine in the aftertaste."

There was an excess of saliva in his mouth, and as he spoke he spat an occasional bright speck of it onto the table.

"Now we can start to eliminate," he said. "You will pardon me for doing this carefully, but there is much at stake. Normally I would perhaps take a bit of a chance, leaping forward quickly and landing right in the middle of the vineyard of my choice. But this time—I must move cautiously this time, must I not?" He looked up at Mike and he smiled, a thick-lipped, wet-lipped smile. Mike did not smile back.

"First, then, which district in Bordeaux does this wine come from? That is not too difficult to guess. It is far too light in the body to be from either St. Emilion or Graves. It is obviously a Médoc. There's no doubt about *that.*

"Now—from which commune in Médoc does it come? That also, by elimination, should not be too difficult to decide. Margaux? No. It cannot be Margaux. It has not the violent bouquet of a Margaux. Pauillac? It cannot be Pauillac, either. It is too tender, too gentle and wistful for a Pauillac. The wine of Pauillac has a character that is almost imperious in its taste. And also, to me, a Pauillac contains just a little pith, a curious, dusty, pithy flavor that the grape acquires from the soil of the district. No, no. This—this is a very gentle wine, demure and bashful in the first taste, emerging shyly but quite graciously in the second. A little arch, perhaps, in the second taste, and a little naughty also, teasing the tongue with a trace, just a trace, of tannin. Then, in the aftertaste, delightful—consoling and feminine, with a certain blithely generous quality that one associates only with the wines of the commune of St. Julien. Unmistakably this is a St. Julien."

He leaned back in his chair, held his hands up level with his chest, and placed the fingertips carefully together. He was becoming ridiculously pompous, but I thought that some of it was deliberate, simply to mock his host. I found myself waiting rather tensely for him to go on. The girl Louise was lighting a cigarette. Pratt heard the match strike and he turned on her, flaring suddenly with real anger. "Please!" he said. "Please don't do that! It's a disgusting habit, to smoke at table!"

She looked up at him, still holding the burning match in one hand, the big slow eyes settling on his face, resting there a moment, moving away again, slow and contemptuous. She bent her head and blew out the match, but continued to hold the unlighted cigarette in her fingers.

"I'm sorry, my dear," Pratt said, "but I simply cannot have smoking at table."

She didn't look at him again.

"Now, let me see—where were we?" he said. "Ah, yes. This wine is from Bordeaux, from the commune of St. Julien, in the district of Médoc. So far, so good. But now we come to the more difficult part—the name of the vineyard itself. For in St. Julien there are many vineyards, and as our host so rightly remarked earlier on, there is often not much difference between the wine of one and the wine of another. But we shall see."

He paused again, closing his eyes. "I am trying to establish the 'growth,'" he said. "If I can do that, it will be half the battle. Now, let me see. This wine is obviously not from a first-growth vineyard—nor even a second. It is not a great wine. The quality, the—the—what do you call it?—the radiance, the power, is lacking. But a third growth—that it could be. And yet I doubt it. We know it is a good year—our host has said so—and this is probably flattering it a little bit. I must be careful. I must be very careful here."

He picked up his glass and took another small sip.

"Yes," he said, sucking his lips, "I was right. It is a fourth growth. Now I am sure of it. A fourth growth from a very good year—from a great year, in fact. And that's what made it taste for a moment like a third—or even a second-growth wine. Good! That's better! Now we are closing in! What are the fourth-growth vineyards in the commune of St. Julien?"

Again he paused, took up his glass, and held the rim against that sagging, pendulous lower lip of his. Then I saw the tongue shoot out, pink and narrow, the tip of it dipping into the wine, withdrawing swiftly again —a repulsive sight. When he lowered the glass, his eyes remained closed, the face concentrated, only the lips moving, sliding over each other like two pieces of wet, spongy rubber.

"There it is again!" he cried. "Tannin in the middle taste, and the quick astringent squeeze upon the tongue. Yes, yes, of course! Now I have it! This wine comes from one of those small vineyards around Beychevelle. I remember now. The Beychevelle district, and the river and the little harbor that has silted up so the wine ships can no longer use it. Beychevelle . . . could it actually be a Beychevelle itself? No, I don't think so. Not quite. But it is somewhere very close. Château Talbot? Could it be Talbot? Yes, it could. Wait one moment."

He sipped the wine again, and out of the side of my eye I noticed Mike Schofield and how he was leaning farther and farther forward over the table, his mouth slightly open, his small eyes fixed upon Richard Pratt.

"No. I was wrong. It was not a Talbot. A Talbot comes forward to you just a little quicker than this one; the fruit is nearer to the surface. If it is a '34, which I believe it is, then it couldn't be Talbot. Well, well. Let me think. It is not a Beychevelle and it is not a Talbot, and yet—yet it is so close to both of them, so close, that the vineyard must be almost in between. Now, which could that be?"

He hesitated, and we waited, watching his face. Everyone, even Mike's wife, was watching him now. I heard the maid put down the dish of vegetables on the sideboard behind me, gently, so as not to disturb the silence.

"Ah!" he cried. "I have it! Yes, I think I have it!"

For the last time, he sipped the wine. Then, still holding the glass up near his mouth, he turned to Mike and smiled, a slow, silky smile, and he said. "You know what this is? This is the little Château Branaire-Ducru."

Mike sat tight, not moving.

"And the year, 1934."

We all looked at Mike, waiting for him to turn the bottle around in its basket and show the label.

"Is that your final answer?" Mike said.

"Yes, I think so."

"Well, is it or isn't it?"

"Yes, it is."

"What was the name again?"

"Château Branaire-Ducru. Pretty little vineyard. Lovely old château. Know it quite well. Can't think why I didn't recognize it at once."

"Come on, Daddy," the girl said. "Turn it round and let's have a peek. I want my two houses."

"Just a minute," Mike said. "Wait just a minute." He was sitting very quiet, bewildered-looking, and his face was becoming puffy and pale, as though all the force was draining slowly out of him.

"Michael!" his wife called sharply from the other end of the table. "What's the matter?"

"Keep out of this, Margaret, will you please."

Richard Pratt was looking at Mike, smiling with his mouth, his eyes small and bright. Mike was not looking at anyone.

"Daddy!" the daughter cried, agonized. "But, Daddy, you don't mean to say he's guessed it right!"

"Now, stop worrying, my dear," Mike said. "There's nothing to worry about."

I think it was more to get away from his family than anything else that Mike then turned to Richard Pratt and said, "I'll tell you what, Richard. I think you and I better slip off into the next room and have a little chat?"

"I don't want a little chat," Pratt said. "All I want is to see the label on that bottle." He knew he was a winner now; he had the bearing, the quiet arrogance of a winner, and I could see that he was prepared to become thoroughly nasty if there was any trouble. "What are you waiting for?" he said to Mike. "Go on and turn it round."

Then this happened: The maid, the tiny, erect figure of the maid in her white-and-black uniform, was standing beside Richard Pratt, holding something out in her hand. "I believe these are yours, sir," she said.

Pratt glanced around, saw the pair of thin horn-rimmed spectacles that she held out to him, and for a moment he hesitated. "Are they? Perhaps they are. I don't know."

"Yes, sir, they're yours." The maid was an elderly woman—nearer seventy than sixty—a faithful family retainer of many years standing. She put the spectacles down on the table beside him.

Without thanking her, Pratt took them up and slipped them into his top pocket, behind the white handkerchief.

But the maid didn't go away. She remained standing beside and slightly behind Richard Pratt, and there was something so unusual in her manner and in the way she stood there, small, motionless, and erect, that I for one found myself watching her with a sudden apprehension. Her old gray face had a frosty, determined look, the lips were compressed, the little chin was out, and the hands were clasped together tight before her. The curious cap on her head and the flash of white down the front of her uniform made her seem like some tiny, ruffled, white-breasted bird.

"You left them in Mr. Schofield's study," she said. Her voice was unnaturally, deliberately polite. "On top of the green filing cabinet in his study, sir, when you happened to go in there by yourself before dinner."

It took a few moments for the full meaning of her words to penetrate, and in the silence that followed I became aware of Mike and how he was slowly drawing himself up in his chair, and the color coming to his face, and the eyes opening wide, and the curl of the mouth, and the dangerous little patch of whiteness beginning to spread around the area of the nostrils.

"Now, Michael!" his wife said. "Keep calm now, Michael, dear! Keep calm!"

Roald Dahl comments on "Taste"

Having read this story to the class, I would say:

Although this one seems to me to be a perfectly straight-forward little tale, the fact remains that it has enjoyed more success and notoriety than any other story I have written. When the manuscript went to *The New Yorker* back in 1949, Harold Ross was so taken with it that he invited me out to lunch at the Algonquin. It had been dramatized for American television at least four separate times, and anthologists, not only in the United States but in most of the European countries, seem drawn toward it like vultures toward a carcass. I myself am thoroughly sick of it by now, but let us nevertheless try to examine it more closely and see if we cannot discover why it has been, and still is, so acceptable nineteen years after it was written.

The plot is a simple one, and could be paraphrased in six lines. If we were to read those six lines before reading the story, we would say simply, "Yes, this is a neat little plot, and it folds itself up nicely at the end, but there doesn't appear to be anything very remarkable about it one way or the other."

At first sight, there isn't. But if the skeleton of the plot is examined carefully, it will be seen to contain scope for an almost unlimited use of what is perhaps the most valuable ingredient of all stories—suspense. If you can create genuine suspense in a story, then the reader is hooked. And if you can prolong that suspense, stretching the elastic out more and more until it looks as though it is going to snap at any moment, then the reader is your slave and he will chase after your words from page to page until you finally release him with an ending. Again, if your suspense is created without any violence at all, as it is in this story, then the effect is more powerful than ever.

This particular plot permits the writer to begin creating suspense very early on. Usually, when one tries to do this, one finds it impossible to maintain that suspense right up to the end, and the result is disastrous. But here the tension is not only maintained all the way through, it is increased, and this is done by having a series of pumping-stations spread out along the route at regular intervals to keep up the pressure. These can be easily picked out:

Pumping-station No. 1. The reader is told that a bet will be made this evening. He also sees a nasty little conflict develop suddenly between the host and the winetaster.

Pumping-station No. 2. The first half of the bet is made. It is important that it be a fantastic one and that it concern a human being (the daughter) rather than merely money. Money alone, or even property and money alone, would have weakened the story 50 per cent. This is an original and unusual bet, and the fact that it is made among conventional people in a conventional setting strengthens the situation.

Pumping-station No. 3. But conventional people (stockbrokers) don't normally accept bets of this kind. What conventional family man, if you please, is going to bet the hand of his daughter in marriage. So this pumping-station is the one where the writer convinces the reader that in *real-life* this conventional man actually would have accepted this unconventional bet. This has to be carefully done, and is the most difficult part of the story. It has to be "possible," otherwise the story will fail.

Pumping-station No. 4. The second half of the bet is made. Here again the bet is unconventional—two houses, a town house and a country house. It is impossible to over-emphasize the importance of being unconventional and surprising in stories of this type. At every turn, the writer must try to substitute the unusual for the usual. And now, already, before we are half way through the story, we have one man betting the hand of his daughter in marriage against another man betting his two houses. The reader, we can be fairly sure, is with us.

Pumping-station No. 5. The slow and infinitely prolonged tasting of the wine, stretched out paragraph by paragraph with a complete change of pace, very very slow, so slow that the reader unconsciously finds himself reading faster and faster to come to the end of it and hear the verdict, and when he does . . .

Pumping-station No. 6. Even when he does, he realizes that this is not the end of the affair. Something else is going to happen. The tension is now considerable. The stockbroker has lost his daughter. The daughter is beside herself. The mother is speechless. But this can't go on. The end must come quickly. The writer recognizes that the suspense or tension cannot be built up any higher.

Pumping-station No. 7. Enter the maid, who reveals obliquely that the winetaster has cheated and is a villain. Stop the story at once. Don't try to go on. Leave the final scene, the dreadful row, the possible act of violence, to the imagination of the reader.

It is interesting to note that this story, whenever it has been performed on television, has failed to come off. You would think it was a natural for TV, but it isn't. And the reason, I think, is that although the plot appears at first sight to be very strong, it is actually rather frail. Its success as a short story is dependent, far more than one would at first think, upon atmosphere—atmosphere and change of pace. You will find, if you examine it closely, comparatively little dialogue. It contains many long descriptive paragraphs, and the television scriptwriter will invariably fill in these pauses with extra dialogue, which is a grave error; for it is in those pauses, those silences, that the tension builds up and the pace changes.

I believe that the only way to produce this story successfully on stage or film would be to take it exactly as it is written, with long pauses and very little dialogue. A French company with a French director has made a short film of Ambrose Bierce's fine story "An Occurrence at Owl Creek Bridge," employing this technique, and the result is magical. I don't think that there are more than half a dozen words spoken in the whole thing. Anyone who gets the chance should go and see it.

PART FOUR

Approaching Short Stories

Characteristically, in teaching students to read fiction, we must keep the story text in front of them and us. But there are times for preliminary-to-reading (or, perhaps, for intermittent-with-reading) exercises, too.

For example, most students leave school (high school *and* college) uncertain about the basic terms of literary criticism. It is difficult to engage in serious talk about literature without using such terms as *theme, tone, symbol, metaphor,* and *structure.* Ideally, definitions should emerge from repeated experiences with stories and be formalized only after such experiences. But that is tomorrow's ideal curriculum, and today tens of thousands of students are being confused by abstract teacher-talk about literature and by imprecise uses of even the most basic terms from the lexicon of literary criticism.

It isn't that we teachers of English (or teachers-of-English-to-be) have no understanding of basic terms. It is rather that our understandings are various. Even such simple terms as *plot* are defined in different ways by critics and teachers. More difficult terms resist *any* precise definition. Indeed, once defined, they take on apparent precision they don't in fact possess (and students infer a false security). For example, if the student looking up *tone* persisted until finding the sixth (and relevant) definition in Webster's, he would read that *tone* is "style or manner of expression in speaking or writing."[1] Not much help. Were he cagey enough to

---

1. *Webster's Seventh New Collegiate Dictionary* (Springfield, Mass.: G. & C. Merriam Co., 1963), p. 931.

look into a specialized handbook, the student might find *more* than he wanted. For example, in the most recent edition of *A Handbook to Literature*,[2] before a paragraph detailing Sidney Lanier's use of *tone* or *tone color*, the student would find:

> *Tone* is used in contemporary criticism, following I. A. Richards' example, as a term designating the attitudes toward the subject and toward the audience implied in a literary work. In such a usage, a work may have a *tone* that is formal, informal, intimate, solemn, sombre, playful, serious, ironic, condescending, or any of many other possible attitudes. Clearly, *tone* in this sense contributes in a major way to the effect and the effectiveness of a literary work.
>
> In another sense, *tone* designates the mood of the work itself and the various devices that are used to create that mood. In this sense, *tone* results from combinations and variations of such things as METER, RIME, ALLITERATION, ASSONANCE, CONSONANCE, DICTION, SENTENCE STRUCTURE REPETITION, IMAGERY, SYMBOLISM, etc.

Surely there is intelligence and experience behind such a definition, but it is not that of most high school students. Even the best student would have difficulty making meaningful contact. Another student might try using the definition without understanding it. For most of us, such abstract definitions open a Pandora's box of confusion.

The teacher's classroom task is to build the student's sense of such terms as *tone* through discussion, through example, and through applications of terms to stories the student is capable of reading. Any seventh-grade class, for example, can distinguish the mood or tone of stories by Poe from those of O. Henry. The teacher's job is to help students say what they know.

Surely the teacher addicted to Friday spelling bees assumes that spelling practice will pay off in student writing. It is more certain that preliminary-to-reading exercises on plot and character will improve the quality of in-class discussion of short stories. Inescapably, our teaching plans must make the vocabulary of—what? —literary criticism a real and working thing.

Preliminary-to-reading exercises can reduce the abstraction of our technical vocabulary. Discussing, challenging, and appraising

---

2. Thrall, Hibbard and Holman (New York: The Odyssey Press, Inc., 1960), p. 487.

is our classroom method: *for* this method, students' control over basic terms is essential; *from* this method, students can infer the flavors and pleasures of good literature.

A preliminary-to-reading exercise: Taste

To "have taste" means to recognize and appreciate high quality. Recognizing quality requires looking at particulars. The following exercise has the certain virtue of requiring a close look at particulars.

Establish with students the notion of "classes" of quality among magazines carrying fiction. For most students, "high-" and "low-" class magazines will be enough—*Harper's*, the *Atlantic Monthly*, *The New Yorker*, say, representing "high-class" magazines, *True Story*, *True Romance*, and *Cavalier* representing "low-class" magazines. For more sophisticated students, classes representing "the slicks" and "the little magazines" might be added.

Collect a wide assortment of excerpts from the different classes of magazines. In collecting excerpts, look for examples of certain aspects of fiction that can be grouped for study. "Story beginnings" might be grouped, for example. The question will be: how interestingly, how skillfully, do these "beginnings" engage the reader? Another set of excerpts might be characterizations. Another set, passages of dialogue. Another, descriptions. Students in one class might help collect and classify excerpts for use in another. And you can reduce to *nil* the chance that students will recognize particular passages by collecting from older issues of magazines.

Here, then, are three "story beginnings." From what class of magazine ("high" or "low") does each of the following come?[3]

Excerpt A

In the office at the garage eight hours a day I wear mauve linen overalls—those snappy uniforms they make for girls who aren't really nurses. I'm forty-nine but I could be twenty-five except for my face, and my legs. I've got that very fair skin and my legs have gone mottled, like Roquefort cheese. My hair used to look pretty as chickens' fluff, but now it's like all that's left of the coat of an old toy animal. It's been bleached and permed too many times. I wouldn't admit this to anyone else, but to

3. Since you are sophisticated readers, it seems fair to try to fool you. But with your own students you should play it straight at the outset. That is, select excerpts you judge to be genuinely representative of the class of magazines they come from.

myself I admit everything. Perhaps I'll get one of those wigs
everyone's wearing. You don't have to be short of hair, any-
more, to wear a wig.

Excerpt B

The golden light had gone from the western mesas and the
shadows had turned to dusk. The small points of the new moon
were cutting the darkness. It was the time, said the Old Ones
of our Hopi tribe, that the night gods came out to guard the
world. I was weary, but sleep wouldn't come. I turned again
in bed and my little sister spoke crossly, "Why do you not
sleep, Felipa?"

Excerpt C

I was shocked, recently, when a neighbor said laughingly of
her thirteen-year-old daughter, "This morning she got flowers
from her boy friend to celebrate their anniversary. They had
their first date just a year ago. Isn't it mad?"

Mad? When I was thirteen, my mother would probably have
called the police at any suggestion of a boy friend, but at that
age no boy looked at me and I looked at no boy. Even when
such exchanges did begin, several years later, and Mother
didn't mind, I was reluctant to bring the boys home; I tried to
keep anybody I liked away from the family as long as I could.
I wanted to keep him to myself . . . .

The first time through, this exercise might be tried chiefly for
fun. But after one trial run, exercises should be prefaced by discussion of what quality in fiction is. For practice, the class might
look at examples in excerpts they have already seen: how good is
the Roquefort cheese simile in Excerpt A, for example? What level
of diction is suggested by the word "mad" in Excerpt C? How precise is the light-shadow-dusk-darkness sequence in Excerpt B? The
general qualities of good fiction are what we know about—what a
good phrase or a full characterization is, what is excessively coin-
cidental, what is sharply concrete and revealing. The point is to
pin down the specific qualities of the excerpt in front of us; this
requires hard talk about single words, phrases, and sentences.

In any case, discussion of appropriate aspects of quality should
precede the second and subsequent exercises. Discussion of what
makes good characterization, for example, should precede the ask-

ing of the overwhelming question, "From what classes of magazines do the following bits of characterization come?"

Excerpt D

I saw the twins, Joanne and Jan, first. Light-haired, brown-eyed, they gave me identical polite greetings. And though grief still lay heavy on their young shoulders, they managed a smile. Petey stood up, Coke bottle in hand, and a taut smile spread across his freckled face. He was tall for his age and much too thin. Joey was huddled near the window, away from the others, his back to the TV set. His woebegone expression tugged my heart.

Steve went over and put his hand on Joey's thin shoulder. "This is Melissa, Joey. She's come to have supper with us. I told her you want to learn to cook spaghetti."

Joey's eyes, blue and round, met mine. Something lurched inside me. And for a moment I was a child again, huddled in a chair, meeting my stepmother for the first time. My heart began a slow, painful beat. I wanted to go to the lonely, heart-broken little boy and comfort him. But the hurt and anger in his small face kept me silent.

Excerpt E

A big bald-headed man with a boil on his chin and a boy in a short-sleeved sweatshirt were sitting on a bench in front of the station. The man was cleaning his fingernails with the leather-punch blade of a Boy Scout knife. It seemed an odd kind of knife for a grown man to have, but you never know with these rednecks. I've never understood them and I never will. They're like a different race. And, of course, he didn't even look up until I slammed the car door. He wiped the blade on his overalls and closed the knife and handed it to the boy. So that, at least, explained that. Then he got up and sauntered across the driveway toward me. He stopped with his hand on the high-test pump, and he had that closed-up look they get. You'd think he'd never seen a Thunderbird before.

Excerpt F

I met Leonie at a skating rink. Or rather, I should say that I just admired her for weeks before I had enough courage to speak to her. She was the most beautiful girl I'd ever seen. She is still the most beautiful girl I've ever seen. It was sheer joy to watch her making figures in her bright, short skating skirt, with her beautiful black hair falling around her shoulders as if it had a life of its own. She always skated by herself, and there was a kind of pride about her for all her friendly smile which made it difficult to come near—more difficult if you were already half in love, as I was.

One evening while she was taking off her skates, she flashed me a breathtaking smile. I noticed a look of loneliness in her smoke-gray eyes, too, and that gave me courage to ask whether I could take her home. Still, I almost fell flat on my face when she accepted. I walked out of that place like a prince with lovely Leonie. What did I care if she'd probably never let me date her for real?[4]

A preliminary-to-reading exercise: Style

Few terms we use in teaching are less precise than *style*. We might dramatize its imprecision by showing how we apply it to literature: we talk about a "writer's style," and mean something like his manner or general concerns or mode, and we talk about "writing style," and have in mind something like the style of his sentences or the linguistic characteristics of his writing. More often, in truth, we mean something fuzzier than either of these.

Neither the style of a writer (a most general thing) nor the style of his writing (by which we can mean his linguistic style) is easy to pin down. A general reference to Thomas Hardy's or John Barth's style connotes the writer's milieu, his themes, moods, and even representative characters. Given a three-hundred-word passage from each (or from Updike and Salinger, say, to remove the telltale signs of the dates of writing), we readily distinguish one from the other.

To make this distinction, we would not need to talk about purely linguistic matters. But if we are going to be precise, if we are going to follow the line of "linguistic style," it is just those matters we must get to: diction, sentence lengths and patterns, "deep" and "surface" structures, and even such particular things as verbal irony or the qualities and amounts of metaphor.

4. As though you didn't know! Excerpt A comes from *Harper's* (November 1964, page 108), excerpt B from *True Romance* (December 1964, page 10), excerpt C from Emily Hahn, "Raymond," *The New Yorker* (August 22, 1964, page 30), excerpt D from *True Story* (December 1964, page 98), excerpt E from Berton Roueché, "A Ride into Town," *The New Yorker* (August 22, 1964, page 96), and excerpt F from *True Romance* (December 1964, pages 4 and 6).

What we do instead is to ask students to write dialogue in the style of Hemingway or to fashion an essay after Lincoln's "Gettysburg Address." We seldom particularize the kinds of stylistic inferences we want students to make in imitating this writer or that. When we do particularize, we reduce "linguistic style" to matters of word choices, sentence patterns (and even sentence lengths), and the quality and extent of metaphor. Well, these things are a start. They are *part* of what style is, but surely not *all* of what it is.

In discussing the style of a sentence, Strunk and White have said it all. Style is what makes "These are the times that try men's souls" a memorable utterance. Other arrangements of the same thought—"Soulwise, these are trying times" or "These are trying times for men's souls"—just aren't durable.[5]

Some distinction between "writer's style" and his "linguistic style" might be made through a conventional kind of writing assignment. The student is given a part of a story and asked to complete it. Let me use one of James Thurber's delightful fables to show how the distinction might be made.

The Princess and the Tin Box

Once upon a time, in a far country, there lived a king whose daughter was the prettiest princess in the world. Her eyes were like the cornflower, her hair was sweeter than the hyacinth, and her throat made the swan look dusty.

From the time she was a year old, the princess had been showered with presents. Her nursery looked like Cartier's window. Her toys were all made of gold or platinum or diamonds or emeralds. She was not permitted to have wooden blocks or china dolls or rubber dogs or linen books, because such materials were considered cheap for the daughter of a king.

When she was seven, she was allowed to attend the wedding of her brother and throw real pearls at the bride instead of rice. Only the nightingale, with his lyre of gold, was permitted to sing for the princess. The common blackbird, with his boxwood flute, was kept out of the palace grounds. She walked in silver-and-samite slippers to a sapphire-and-topaz bathroom and slept in an ivory bed inlaid with rubies.

On the day the princess was eighteen, the king sent a royal ambassador to the courts of five neighboring kingdoms to announce that he would give his daughter's hand in marriage to the prince who brought her the gift she liked the most.

The first prince to arrive at the palace rode a swift white stallion and laid at the feet of the princess an enormous apple made of solid gold which

5. William Strunk and E. B. White, *The Elements of Style*, (New York: The Macmillan Company, 1959), p. 53.

he had taken from a dragon who had guarded it for a thousand years. It was placed on a long ebony table set up to hold the gifts of the princess's suitors. The second prince, who came on a gray charger, brought her a nightingale made of a thousand diamonds, and it was placed beside the golden apple. The third prince, riding on a black horse, carried a great jewel box made of platinum and sapphires, and it was placed next to the diamond nightingale. The fourth prince, astride a fiery yellow horse, gave the princess a gigantic heart made of rubies and pierced by an emerald arrow. It was placed next to the platinum-and-sapphire jewel box.

Now the fifth prince was the strongest and handsomest of all the five suitors, but he was the son of a poor king whose realm had been overrun by mice and locusts and wizards and mining engineers so that there was nothing much of value left in it. He came plodding up to the palace of the princess on a plow horse and he brought her a small tin box filled with mica and feldspar and hornblende which he had picked up on the way.

The other princes roared with disdainful laughter when they saw the tawdry gift the fifth prince had brought to the princess. But she examined it with great interest and squealed with delight, for all her life she had been glutted with precious stones and priceless metals, but she had never seen tin before or mica or feldspar or hornblende. The tin box was placed next to the ruby heart pierced with an emerald arrow.

"Now," the king said to his daughter, "you must select the gift you like best and marry the prince that brought it."

Students asked to complete the fable, emulating Thurber's "linguistic style," would need to observe certain linguistic characteristics. There are the similes early in the fable; there is the choice of images (e.g., "rubber dogs," or "mica or feldspar or hornblende," or "sapphire-and-topaz bathroom") that set up a jangle between the modern world and "a far country" of long ago; there are the syntactic parallels (e.g., the nightingale and blackbird sentences of paragraph three, the pattern established in introducing the four princes in paragraph five); there is the lush concrete imagery of the princes' gifts and the diction that marks the differences between the "have" princes and the poor "have not" (e.g., the "swift white stallion" and the "fiery yellow horse" against the plodding plow horse). In this case the students' success in the assignment would depend on how well he tuned in to the linguistic characteristics of Thurber's fable.

If the student had instead been asked to complete the fable in the "manner" or "fashion" of Thurber, another set of cues would predominate. You would help him remember Thurber's persistent championing of the male animal in his cartoons and stories—in "The Secret Life of Walter Mitty," in "The Catbird Seat," and in the stage production *A Thurber Carnival*. They would be reminded of

Thurber's satire and irony, his insistence upon the unexpected, his abrasive juxtapositioning of modern society and ancient times, of dream worlds where men are heroes and of real worlds where they are puny.

In this case the students would know exactly which prince the princess chose. You can prove this certainty to yourself by writing two conclusions, before reading Thurber's own, one emulating his "manner" and the other his "linguistic style." And whether you succeed or fail altogether, you will be reminded that having students complete the story of a professional is a sure-fire way to get some writing from them.

Well, what did you do with the story? Here's what Thurber did.

The princess smiled and walked up to the table and picked up the present she liked the most. It was the platinum-and-sapphire jewel box, the gift of the third prince.

"The way I figure it," she said, "is this. It is a very large and expensive box, and when I am married, I will meet many admirers who will give me precious gems with which to fill it to the top. Therefore, it is the most valuable of all the gifts my suitors have brought me and I like it the best."

The princess married the third prince that very day in the midst of great merriment and high revelry. More than a hundred thousand pearls were thrown at her and she loved it.

Moral: All those who thought the princess was going to select the tin box filled with worthless stones instead of one of the other gifts will kindly stay after class and write one hundred times on the blackboard "I would rather have a hunk of aluminum silicate than a diamond necklace."

If you chose to emulate Thurber's "manner," and if you remembered enough about him, you chose any prince but number five for your conclusion: In Thurber's world, prince number five must stand aside while one of his well-fixed rivals wins the princess whose world has been essentially material. (The little gold-digger!) If you attempted emulation of Thurber's linguistic style, your success depended not upon the "right" *conclusion* but on the right *sentences*. Is there something of Thurber in what you wrote? Are there figures, uses of fairy-tale convention and the cliché fairy-tale plot, sentences that have "Thurberian" balance, rhythm, and ring?

Some useful talk about *style* might come out of an assignment involving emulation. Of course, in the case of Thurber, no young student should be made to feel foolish because he "chose the wrong prince." But you can discuss with him why he chose the prince he did or wrote the sentences he did. The main joke of the fable is the princess' realistic appraisal of the world up against the reader's romantic expectations for the fairy tale. Understanding style requires discussion and close examination of texts; completion exercises may provide either or both.

A preliminary-to-reading exercise: Structure

Today's young person is used to chaos in life; he probably hasn't thought much about form and order. A good short story is one answer to the buzzing, howling confusion that he knows too well. A good short story is arranged better than life, and students can be helped to see the order and pattern in fiction.

The sentence provides an analog for considering structure, or *pattern.* If you put on the chalkboard the word *The,* and ask students to supply a word that might follow it, you're likely to be offered a noun. Put the noun, say *cucumber,* an inviting distance from the *The:*

The   cucumber

Then, of course, students might be asked what will fall between the two words; they might offer *cool* and then, with *cool* near the *cucumber, deliciously: The deliciously cool cucumber . . . .* If the class is afflicted with the need to predicate, let them: *The deliciously cool cucumber oozed with flavor.* (Kids always choose *ooze!*) The point of this is to introduce the notion of available options: Once *The deliciously cool . . .* is established, the next word must be selected from a finite pool of possibilities. And once *cucumber* is added, possibilities for what will come next are further limited.

This principle works in stories, too: options decrease as the story progresses from relative formlessness to meaning. A very short story might prove the notion. Using Björnstjerne Björnson's "The Father,"[6] we work toward a sense of structure from inferences about the commitments being made.

The Father

The man whose story is here to be told was the wealthiest and most influential person in his parish; his name was Thord Overaas. He appeared in the priest's study one day, tall and earnest.

6. *75 Short Masterpieces,* Bantam Books, pages 24-27.

What expectancies does the title establish? What do we know of the father (as to appearance, demeanor, and position) and the scene? Is the father in the priest's office to seek spiritual guidance? At this point the options are numerous, but already limitations are established in character and setting. We speculate a while, ruling out irrelevant ideas and supporting those that come out of the text.

We might next consider paragraphs two through six. (An opaque projector is helpful for an exercise of this kind.)

"I have gotten a son," said he, "and I wish to present him for baptism."

"What shall his name be?"

"Finn—after my father."

"And the sponsors?"

They were mentioned, and proved to be the best men and women of Thord's relations in the parish.

The purpose of Thord's visit is set. He has just become a father and wishes to arrange for his son's baptism. We infer his pride in family and position: he provides worthy sponsors. Now, we ask, where might the story be leading? What possibilities exist at this point? What relationship exists between priest and father? Any hints as to relationship between father and son? We encourage text-rooted speculation from the sparse statements available. And when speculation runs dry, we expose more text.

"Is there anything else?" inquired the priest, and looked up.

The peasant hesitated a little.

"I should like very much to have him baptized by himself," said he, finally.

"That is to say on a week-day?"

"Next Saturday, at twelve o'clock noon."

"Is there anything else?" inquired the priest.

Now there's a bit more to chew on. Thord wants his son baptized alone—isolated from other children. For what possible reason? Pride? Is there something about the circumstances of birth Thord wants to hide? Is there something wrong with the boy? We talk and then yield a bit more of the text.

"There is nothing else"; and the peasant twirled his cap, as though he were about to go.

Then the priest rose. "There is yet this, however," said he, and walking toward Thord, he took him by the hand and looked gravely into his eyes: "God grant that the child may become a blessing to you!"

One day sixteen years later, Thord stood once more in the priest's study.

It would probably be wise to lead students to the understanding that Thord is wrong in thinking "There is nothing else," for Thord is back, sixteen years later, and we can assume now that he is back to take up another matter concerning his son. What might it be? We will stop here, with the peeling off of the story, and make the point. As the story proceeds, a clear pattern emerges: the story consists largely of episodes between the priest and Thord, each episode marking a point of development in the boy's life. After the second encounter, during which Thord arranges for his son's confirmation, the episode again closes with Thord's "There is nothing else." The third episode occurs when Thord comes to the priest to arrange for the publishing of banns for his son's marriage to "the richest girl in the parish." And at the conclusion of that episode, Thord says, "But now I am through with him."

The pattern of the story thus far suggests a nice structural problem, for the order of the story is a series of visits between father and priest; each is concluded by Thord in a definitive way: "There is nothing else." Yet the story shows that each time there *is* "something else." Will the visits continue? Does Thord's "But now I am through with him" suggest that a different kind of visit is coming? What possibilities exist?

The structural pattern of "The Father," what it reveals and how it progressively limits what *can* occur next, the repetitions of language and the growing revelation of character, are there for scrutiny. Students will enjoy considering or analyzing how stories establish commitments and fulfill them. Detective work is fun and, on occasion, instructive.

Sounds in fiction

Aloud and silently aloud: Hearing short stories. Once a student learns to read, the greatest single block to his enjoyment of fiction is that he doesn't *hear* much of anything. He doesn't hear voices singing and rasping, praising and ridiculing, sweet-talking and sneering, chuckling and guffawing. Voices in literature do these and many more things—and not just those voices in dialogue. A key breakthrough in teaching a foreign language is to get the student to *think* in the language he is learning; a key breakthrough in the teaching of short stories is to get the student to *hear* the stories he is reading. When he is able to hear, such abstractions as tone, characterization, irony, humor, and setting may begin to make sense.

Most readers (and I include adult readers here) never learn to listen to written words. Words remain on the page, inert. That they are symbols of sound is a well-known but ignored fact. Long before writing to Jack Schaefer and asking him to write a piece for this book, I intended to make a case for helping students get the written words off the page and into the ear. Schaefer has convincingly argued this necessity (See pp. 45–77). Here, then, I'll discuss how the teacher can help students hear the written words.

It might do to talk with students about the sounds of fiction. Much of the vocabulary used to talk about prose fiction is also applied to dramatic fiction; discussion of sound in prose fiction might begin with some parallels and differences. When drama is performed, actors interpret through gesture, movement, and tone of voice. Unless an effort is made in the classroom to get drama off the page, unless students read aloud (and even move about to do some primitive "blocking out" of scene and action), drama might just as well be taught as prose fiction. The significant generic difference between drama and prose fiction is that in drama the actors—the mediators—interpret for the audience. The job of the reader of prose fiction is to perform as actor *and* audience. He must both make the voices of characters come alive *and* listen to the sounds that are made. If he can go farther—if he can create in imagination the way a character looks and moves, can visualize the settings for the action, and if he can listen to the author as well, he will be getting from prose most of its dramatic qualities.

At the outset, then, I recommend a great deal of reading aloud —of "oral interpretation," even. Before students are asked to read a story at home and then "do something" with it—answer questions, write character sketches, or identify its theme—passages from the story should be read aloud. Especially in junior-high classes, preliminary readings-aloud should be your own—carefully prepared to demonstrate something of the sound of a particular passage. Students should be brought into the act very early, but the key here is to have them prepare their readings toward a specific end: finding a paragraph of narration and reading it at an appropriate pace would be one example. Is the narration quick and staccato (as in Liam O'Flaherty's "The Sniper") or slow and mood-making (as in Edgar Allan Poe's "The Fall of the House of Usher")? Scenes of dialogue prepared carefully for reading aloud is another appropriate preliminary-to-reading activity.

Toward the goal of preparing students to read well *independently,* professionally produced recordings of stories have only limited value.[7] Ultimately, you want to teach students to "read aloud silently" or "silently aloud." If you can get students to believe surely enough that *hearing* a story is one of the great pleasures of reading, they will learn to hear dialogue spoken by individual characters and to hear a variety of tones; they may learn to hear relationships between the rhythm of the language and what is going on in the story.

I watched and admired what happened when one teacher recorded three students reading aloud selected passages of narration from Thomas Wolfe, J. D. Salinger, and Joseph Conrad. After the taping, done in class in front of all students, the teacher played the readings back at half speed. Only a few words could be distinguished, but that there are rhythms in prose and that rhythms can be distinguished one from another was convincingly established. Once the generalizations about what they had heard emerged, students looked with greater interest at the relation between form and content.

The sound of language is important to the craft of fiction and a source of delight to many who play with it. Playing with voices and rhythms may revive in students what usually lies dormant: a delight in word music. Exercises can be overdone. We need to get to the reading of whole stories before the year has slipped by. But a variety of exercises, most of them dealing with short passages culled from stories yet to be assigned, may have a real payoff. First exercises in sound, probably, should be the reading aloud of passages of conventional dialogues. Ultimately, the pace, tones, and voices of an entire story might be considered.

Voices in "The Secret Life of Walter Mitty."   One problem with the written word is that it gets between the reader and language. This paradoxical statement suggests a truth: as long as students see written statements simply as conveyers of information (and as long as we teachers consider such information to have an existence independent of the language which embodies it), students

7. They are, in a sense, too good: a given interpretation is inescapable; their professional "theatricality" is beyond the ability of most young readers. But an excerpt, say, of "The Tell-Tale Heart," might usefully set up a model for student emulation without intimidating or stifling students with its competence.

are tacitly encouraged to think of language as an unfortunate but necessary nuisance. We might instead encourage students to think of language as the sounds people make when they talk.

James Thurber's "The Secret Life of Walter Mitty" is a likely subject for investigation of sound. Everyone knows the story of the fantasy life of that timid little Thurberesque man. The story begins with Walter playing, in his mind, the role of a Navy flyer:

> "We're going through!" The Commander's voice was like thin ice breaking. He wore his full-dress uniform, with the heavily braided white cap pulled down rakishly over one cold gray eye. "We can't make it, sir. It's spoiling for a hurricane, if you ask me." "I'm not asking you, Lieutenant Berg," said the Commander. "Throw on the power lights! Rev her up to 8,500! We're going through!"

Have students consider the dialogue alone:

> THE COMMANDER. We're going through!
> LT. BERG. We can't make it, sir. It's spoiling for a hurricane, if you ask me.
> THE COMMANDER. I'm not asking you, Lieutenant Berg. Throw on the power lights! Rev her up to 8,500! We're going through!

Have two of your students read the parts aloud. Give them no preliminary instruction: simply let them have a go at it. You may get a good reading or a bad one. No matter—whichever way the reading comes out is all right. If it is a good reading, let the class discuss its merits. If it is inadequate, let the class point out what is lacking. Does the Commander speak with a voice "like thin ice breaking"? What tonal qualities does such a "stage direction" imply? What does it imply about the situation? What does the content of Lt. Berg's statement tell about his reaction to the situation? How will he speak under stress of this sort? What will be the Commander's tone when he responds to the Lieutenant? Is he afraid? Fearless? How will his voice alter as he shifts from reprimanding his weak-spined subordinate to giving orders? What will he sound like as a leader among men, giving inspiration to his faltering crew?

This same first paragraph supplies an example of a rhetoric familiar to all young devotees of the late, late movie:

> The Commander stared at the ice forming on the pilot window. He walked over and twisted a row of complicated dials. "Switch

on No. 8 auxiliary!" he shouted. "Switch on No. 8 auxiliary!"
repeated Lieutenant Berg. "Full strength in No. 3 turret!"
shouted the Commander. "Full strength in No. 3 turret!" The
crew, bending to their various tasks in the huge, hurtling
eight-engined Navy hydroplane, looked at each other and
grinned. "The Old Man'll get us through," they said to one
another. "The Old Man ain't afraid of Hell!"

Berg, subordinating his personal feelings and becoming a part
of a well-oiled machine, assumes another voice. The reader must
hear that difference, should grasp the crisp, military tone of the
young officer. The effectiveness of the Old Man's persuasiveness,
his reputation as hero, should be evident in the admiring, servile
tones of the crew.

Into this dream world break the strident sounds of Mrs. Mitty,
who sits beside the real Walter Mitty as they make their down-to-
earth way to Waterbury, Connecticut:

"Not so fast! You're driving too fast! . . . What are you driving
so fast for?"

What is the immediate image the students get of this marital relationship? How does Mrs. Mitty handle poor Walter? What tone of
voice does she use with him? Later on, she orders him to get a pair
of overshoes for himself; he replies: "I don't need overshoes." How
will he say that? Straight Milquetoast style? Will some of the military bearing of his fantasy world trail over into reality? Will it take
time for Commander Mitty to subside into henpecked husband
with "the roaring of the SN202 through the worst storm in twenty
years of Navy flying fading in the remote, intimate airways of
his mind"?

Examples of rhythms. The author's telling of a story is made
possible by—and is limited by—words. Not words singly, although
single words can be significant, but clusters of words, strings of
words, words in narration and description and dialect.

Before we can bring students to the kind of sound-awareness
they need to develop, we should consider the affective quality of
sound as we experience it. We must make ourselves as sensitive
to sound as possible. Let's consider some effects of rhythm.

Listen, for instance, to the first paragraph of Hemingway's
"The Undefeated":

Manuel Garcia climbed the stairs to Don Miguel Retana's office. He set down his suitcase and knocked on the door. There was no answer. Manuel, standing in the hallway, felt there was someone in the room. He felt it through the door.

There we have the essence of much of Hemingway—the simple sentence recurring with tempered predictability, the characteristic movement from subject to predicate with a single, hardly noticeable exception in the fourth sentence, the nominals stripped of all but minimal modification. The words themselves, except for "office," the participial "standing," and proper names, are monosyllables or compoundings of monosyllables: "suitcase," "someone." The unobtrusive, restrained quality of the lines is fully in keeping with Hemingway's preoccupations: uneffusive manliness; the muted pathos of the Hemingway hero, undefeated in the face of inevitable defeat, uncomplaining and doomed. The latent sound of the printed word announces the starkness of human experience as Hemingway reveals it. But even for Hemingway and the world he creates there come times when the tempo heightens, when the hero palpitates at the nearness of triumph or despair. Notice the way the shape and the sound of the sentence alter. The simple sentence remains, but a rhythmic complexity is created in layers of modification as the picador, Zurito, and Manuel await the approaching bull:

> Zurito sat there, his feet in the box-stirrups, his great legs in the buckskin-covered armor gripping the horse, the reins in his left hand, the long pic held in his right hand, his broad hat well down over his eyes to shade them from the lights, watching the distant door of the toril.

Meanwhile, in the stands, the critic for *El Heraldo*—the second-string critic—writes in his notebook in a pseudolearned jargon: "the veteran Manolo designed a series of acceptable veronicas, ending in a very Belmontistic recorte that earned applause from the regulars, and we entered the tercio of the cavalry." The reader must try to hear the tone of that utterance: the condescension—the facile, unfeeling, cheaply worn competence of the hack in the presence of tragedy. But when we come back to a view of the essential drama itself, back to the center of it where the pain is so acute that it must be understated, we return to the simple, unmodulated cadences of the opening paragraph. Manuel, mortally wounded, lies on the operating table.

Manuel lay back. They had put something over his face. It was all familiar. He inhaled deeply. He felt very tired. He was very, very tired. They took the thing away from his face.

In contrast to Hemingway, consider the extravagant mixture of vulgate idiom and pomposity in the language of the kidnaper-narrator of O. Henry's "The Ransom of Red Chief":

Bill and me had a joint capital of about six hundred dollars and we needed just two thousand dollars more to pull off a fraudulent town-lot scheme in Western Illinois with. We talked it over on the front steps of the hotel. Philoprogenitiveness, says we, is strong in semi-rural communities; therefore, and for other reasons, a kidnapping project ought to do better there than in the radius of newspapers that send reporters out in plain clothes to stir up talk about such things. We knew that Summit couldn't get after us with anything stronger than constables and, maybe, some lackadaisical bloodhounds and a diatribe or two in the *Weekly Farmers' Budget.* So, it looked good.

Nobody really *reads* this story until he senses the mixed-up cadences of the narration: the juxtapositions of the vulgate ("Bill and me had" and "says we") against the sprinkling of polysyllabics; the fairly longish, formal-level sentences against the short, colloquial sentence. He must sense, too, the sound of the scornful city boy who recalls a time when he was about to take in the country boobs—both scorn and self-mockery.

To catch the bitter irony of D. H. Lawrence's "The Rocking-Horse Winner," one must see through the apparent simplicity, the folk tale clarity, and the never-never-land rhythms of the opening sentences. Their deceptive repetitions in words and syntax offer, quite falsely, happily-ever-after-solutions. The opening passage of the story could be arranged like a poem:

There was a woman who was beautiful,
          who started with all the advantages,
               yet she had no luck.
She married for love,
          and the love turned to dust.
She had bonny children,
          yet she felt they had been thrust upon her,
          and she could not love them.

Playing with "poetic" prose in this fashion may bring students to an awareness of sound in fiction. Certainly just telling them it is there won't work. We must begin with whatever potential they may have for grasping the concepts we wish them to make their own. Some teachers of real ingenuity may be able to bring in records by the Beatles or Simon and Garfunkel and help students draw relevant parallels.

The classroom should be the place where students can investigate rhythms in prose. Rather than pointing out the beauties of language, the teaching trick is to help students ask, and perhaps answer, how a language is in accord with the elements of plot, of setting, of characterization, of theme. It is a case of bringing conscious listening to the silent voices that speak to readers. It is certain (and demonstrable in a laboratory) that the printed word, lying inertly on the page, even when read silently, changes to sound through some mysterious physiology of inner ear and throat muscles.

How can we approach this consciousness and yet avoid simple-minded gush? Perhaps we can speak to seventh-graders of "smooth" and "rough" sentences. They might be asked to classify some sentences as smooth or rough (or as neither) and see whether they can identify what contributes to smoothness or roughness. More advanced students may be able to approach prose rhythms through syntax. Grammar is a formative force in sentence-making. What syntactic patterns are established? What variations from these patterns does the author use? What effects do the departures create? Later, some primitive phonemic elements—the analyzable sound of words—could be isolated.

The question is *not* "What was Thomas Wolfe trying to do here?" but "What did Wolfe achieve by patterning his sentences as he did?" What did he achieve by selecting this word for this slot? By using this metaphor? That crescendo of "harsh consonants"? Such questions are not worth asking all the time. Certainly they should not be asked of every story. But the true story will get some of its truth from its rhythms and tones.

What each of these devices suggests is the combination of a close look with the eye and a careful reading aloud with the voice. The desired end of any analysis is to affect the silent reader with the order and the sound of words: reading aloud with an eye to roughness, for example; reading aloud a series of sentences of one syntactic pattern and comparing them to a set of another pattern; reading aloud some richly textured passages in which definite sound systems are at work. Such reading is done for an understanding of the effects of sound.

Plot

One might say (and be forever sorry he had said it) that there are two kinds of plot. The first is definite, observable, and can even be diagrammed by teachers gifted in chalkboard art. This kind of plot line answers the question of "who did what to whom and with what consequences." For example, this is the line that settles whether Richard Pratt, in "Taste," will win or lose his bet. In terms of the reader's interest in narrative, in "how things turn out," this is the more important kind of plot.

The second kind of plot is an inference from what is presented about people in a situation. This plot often comes from theme— from the aspect of human experience the writer wants his story to comment on. This psychological plot, the working out of the action in terms of its effects upon character, settles not "what happened to whom" so much as it reveals the effects of what happened.

Such stories as "Taste," "Jacob," and—to a lesser degree— "The Chaser" are examples of stories satisfying both the explicit and psychological dimensions of plot. "Appointment with Love" satisfies the requirements of explicit plot; "After You, My Dear Alphonse" satisfies the psychological plot.

In discussing plot—either explicit or implicit—we are talking in metaphor. Plot is not the story; it is like the story in some ways. The metaphor young readers most need to comprehend is the explicit plot design; without understanding of it, the psychological dimensions lurking beneath remain only partly grasped, much less understood.

Explicit plot. Basically, explicit plot presents a question or issue and then answers or resolves it. Because of the question or issue, the reader's attention is focused on what the story is about. Explicit narrative plot satisfies the natural human curiosity about what happened: the more artful the plot, the more satisfying the relief from the itch of curiosity about what happened.

Although there are notable differences between the traditional short story and the modern short story—the first heavily plotted, the latter almost plotless in contrast—both can be talked about in terms of a beginning, a skewed-toward-the-conclusion middle, and the end itself; problem, turning point, and resolution is another set of terms for the same progression. Students will need experience with even so simple a metaphor if it is to illuminate understanding. Begin with something simple:

> Johnny was late coming from school. Mrs. Wocjik heard the front door slam and then watched Johnny come into the kitchen. He pushed his books angrily onto the counter. "No more," he said, looking straight at his mother. "They aren't going to do that any more. And you aren't either."

This beginning makes some guarantees. Conflict or tension is posed, and the reader can expect the story to deal with this conflict. If the story that follows is artistically whole, Johnny's conflict with someone outside his family (perhaps with teachers or authorities at school) and the echo of that conflict (at home, probably with his mother) will be settled somehow. The subject matter of the conflict is not established, but there are hundreds of subjects that are *not* likely to follow this particular beginning: an intrigue among Parisian fashion designers, for example; what happened to sister Susie during her YWCA camp experience, for another. The story beginning promises that something has been *done* to Johnny. At least he thinks so. We expect to find out what that something is and, further, what is done about it.

Story beginnings have a key plot function: they help the reader focus on who, what, and where. This can be understood by young readers. Put in front of them a half dozen story beginnings:

What is this story going to be about?
What is it *not* going to be about?
What kind of problem or tension might develop?
In what situation is this story placed?

Turning point and climax are near synonyms. The turning point is where the presentation of conflict ends and solution begins, but it is not the solution itself. In a heavily plotted story like "Taste," Dahl signals the turning point:

> Then this happened: The maid, the tiny, erect figure of the maid in her white-and-black uniform, was standing beside Richard Pratt, holding something out in her hand. "I believe these are yours, sir," she said.

The tension of "Taste" is complete at this point. The question of whether Pratt will win the bet has been fully posed. The story now needs to provide answer and explanation. But note that the explanation isn't here in the turning point: the *deus-ex-machina* maid breaks the tension with her intrusion, and we know that what she holds in her hand relates to the issue which is in—but has not completed—the process of working out.

In the lightly plotted "After You, My Dear Alphonse," the turning point comes when it is finally clear to Mrs. Wilson that Boyd simply won't behave as she expects him to:

> ". . . Suppose before you leave I make up a big bundle and then you and Johnny can take it over to your mother right away . . ." Her voice trailed off as she saw Boyd's puzzled expression.

As opposed to "Taste," where it is clear within two paragraphs that in Richard Pratt's expertise lies the issue of the story, the issue of "After You, My Dear Alphonse" is slow to develop. It is a subtler issue than that of "Taste." The central tension of "After You, My Dear Alphonse" is between Mrs. Wilson's expectations and Boyd's behavior and situation. When Mrs. Wilson sees that Boyd won't behave "properly," the issue is at maximum tension. Now we want to know how the characters will react to the impasse. Mrs. Wilson, hurt by Boyd's final "rebuff," behaves childishly. That's appropriate, since her expectations are childish. Boyd and Johnny behave pretty much as they have all along. Boyd is on the edge of learning something ("Boyd stood for a minute, staring at Mrs. Wilson's back"), but all he gets is confirmation of the fact of life that all children learn sometime: mothers *are* "screwy" sometimes.

The main question about the turning point isn't *where* in the story it comes, although this question can vex anyone who wants to point to the very syllable at which the tension is highest. But that's more a geographic than an artistic issue. The artistic question is whether the conflict or problem is still present, is relevant to the turning point. Students should be given enough to infer that a *good* story does have a turning point that resolves the problem:

> Has the turning point to do with the established conflict or problem?
>
> Is the conflict fully developed at this point?
>
> Does the turning point solve the conflict or only promise a solution? If the latter, is the promise "satisfying"?

The quality of the conclusion can be discussed. Is the working out reasonable in terms of the story? In terms of "life"? Does it somehow satisfy the problem or conflict posed in the story? The turning point of a story implies that there will be consequences; the conclusion, or denouement, provides them. In the traditional story, the consequences are usually (and necessarily) the fitting together of plot elements. This does not imply "a happy ending," of course, but it does imply the tying together of the plot strings. "Appointment with Love" satisfies this necessity with considerable ingenuity. In the modern short story, consequences are often implied; they characteristically involve the effects on people of what has happened; that is, the resolution is as much one of character as of plot. Characters are changed or unchanged by what has occurred; relationships among people are different; a character has discovered something about life, and he must adjust to that discovery somehow. The consequences on the narrator in "Jacob" illustrate this last situation.

Plot and character provide young readers with dimensions of fiction they can learn to handle. Plot and character are subject to analysis by young readers, and most of them need practice in analysis. Any effort at plot analysis ultimately becomes an exercise in metaphor: the analysis is not the plot itself. Keeping the metaphor simple is the essential thing.

Beginning-middle-end analysis is oversimplification but serviceable as a place to begin. Both traditional and modern stories characteristically demonstrate conflict or issue, turning point, and resolution. If a more elaborate analytical theory seems appropriate, the classical five-part scheme might satisfy: the first stage of the five-part plot presents the conflict or problem to be solved; the second stage complicates that conflict; the third stage brings it to climax; the fourth explores the implications of choice at the climax; and the fifth presents the resolution. Such a breakdown wouldn't be a bad refinement for students to learn—if they were taught it through examples and discussion.

Implicit plot.   Most artful stories can be read on both explicit and implicit levels: enough happens "on the page" to satisfy the plot appetite of every reader; the reader whose psychological appetite has been whetted can satisfy that too, although he is less certain of what it is that is satisfying him. Poor stories have only winners—of ball games, of gun fights, of girls. A poor story poses a tension between two boys and solves it by having the family of one boy move from Sioux Falls to Phoenix. But what has *really* happened? What forces or characteristics or value systems in the two boys have been modified? The causes of tension remain in the characters and, ostensibly, will be tested again. In a sense, the story has not been written.

The implied or psychological structure of plot cannot be diagramed (nor even talked about very surely). Many stories settle the explicit problems raised at their beginnings by resolving those literal conflicts: a tension develops and is ostensibly resolved, a showdown develops and "winners" and "losers" emerge. Pratt will either name the precise château from which the claret came, or he won't; Mrs. Wilson will gain understanding from the innocent boys, or she will not. In neither of these cases is the resolution really germane. These are the resolutions of literal tensions. But we are more interested in seeing Pratt *defeated,* whether he names the château or fails; we care more about Jacob's dignity and about the white man's ignorance than about Jacob's survival. We want confirmation of Mrs. Wilson's ignorance, so Johnny and Boyd can continue in innocence. These are issues of the implicit (or psychological) plot.

Psychological plot is at the intersection of structure and theme. Explicit plot can (and should) be talked about: Have we got the literal things straight? Exactly what happened here? But most serious stories have an issue or theme beyond the literal issue, and it is that issue or theme we want to discuss with students eventually. For young readers, talk about psychological plot defies precision. Yet we do want to talk about what the story is *really* about. Thus chalkboard diagrams, a useful visual art for reducing the abstraction of many a classroom metaphor, may hide the real *issue* in a short story.

The psychological structure of a story creates an appetite and (in a good story) satisfies it. The real issue is often not how the narrative problem is resolved but how the psychological dilemma is resolved. The ostensible satisfactions (whether Pratt guesses the right château, whether Jacob lives or dies, how Mrs. Wilson will react after Boyd's final refusal, whether Alan's love potion will work) are subordinate to the psychological satisfactions (whether Mrs. Wilson will "reform" somehow, whether Alan will be able to handle the consequences of his naïveté). What we care about in "Haircut" is what kind of man Jim Kendall really is; clearly he isn't just what the words on the page say he is.

Discovering aesthetic design may be the deepest pleasure the reading of fiction offers. This is the pleasure of intellectual activity, of discovering and understanding what is going on in a created world. Discovering and understanding amount finally to learning not the "message" or the moral but what in the fiction is artistically satisfying and psychologically important.

Characterization

One of our responsibilities is to help students arrive at some sense of how characterization is achieved—the ways or system of characterization. That characters are revealed by *how* they speak, by *what* they say, by *how* they act, by *what* other characters say about them, etc., is rather widely discussed or "taught" in school classrooms. But these "ways" are neither perfectly understood nor do they reveal the whole truth of characterization.

Pleasure is one of our aims in helping students read fiction. One kind of pleasure comes from being "in" on what's happening. The reader who can see how an author is going about characterizing may derive this kind of pleasure. Some sense of the system of characterization can be arrived at inductively—that is, by looking hard at stories and seeing how characters are built.

What are some of the things we can do to tune students in to methods of characterization? We can, first, start with things they know. The people students know in real life fall into classes or types. To classify in one way, there are the people they know fully, whose personalities they are familiar with, whose actions they can predict from familiarity. There are less well-known people encountered in the jobs (policeman, shopkeeper) or roles (authoritarian) they perform. There are myriad people who more or less "occupy space" on occasion: the man who comes to the door, the lady who passes on the street. Students see the "outsides" of these people, and may hear them speak or watch as they perform somehow, but they may know nothing about their personalities.

These same classes of characters exist in short stories. Students need to know how these classes function artistically.

A first preliminary-to-reading exercise, then, might get students to think and talk about the "classes" of people they know in life and will encounter in stories. In applying their knowledge of "real life" characters to stories, students will inevitably discard the simplistic view that fiction offers two kinds of characterizations— the "good" characters that are fully developed and "round" and the "bad" characters that are underdeveloped, thin, and stereotypical. In short, students apply to stories what they know of the spectrum of characters in the real world.

A somewhat more sophisticated notion of characterization might be based on the rhetorical notion of "distance" between minor characters and main characters. I saw what seemed to me a very useful primitive discussion of "distance" in one tenth-grade classroom. First, the class settled details of plot—what happened to whom and why. Then the story's three main characters were listed on the board. One by one, every other character appearing in the story was discussed. The relation of the minor characters to the main characters (and to the main story line) were considered as the minor characters were discussed. Students were asked to locate them relatively close to or far from the main characters. No two minor characters were equidistant; each was relatively "close to" or "farther from" the story's central concerns.

A somewhat more complicated way of considering "distances" among characters is to start with a simple plot line and ask students to "people" the plot with perhaps a dozen characters who might be somehow involved. Let's say a story begins with a man's subway trip from home to office. The problem is that during the trip he has to reach a decision whether to stay with or quit a company that has asked him to do something unethical. There's our "story line," thin as it is, and our "conflict." We ask students what characters are needed to develop the story. One student suggests that we might include (via flashback) what happened when a close friend of the protagonist faced a similar decision and decided to do the "right" thing, despite what it "cost" him. Another student suggests that the narration stop for just a minute and focus on a faceless fellow passenger on the subway train who somehow symbolizes integrity to the protagonist: it's the man's "look," or the man's "style." Another student, caught up in our exciting narrative, reminds us of the protagonist's young son, who recently faced a moral dilemma. Wouldn't the protagonist remember the sanctimonious advice he gave his son? Another student tells us of the protagonist's boss, who has posed the unethical dilemma. All together, students suggest eight or ten characters who might be involved in the story. Which of these require thorough characterization? Which require less thorough characterization? Which require nothing more than a gender (male) or a look (worried) or a characteristic (courage)? Remind students of the space limits of the short story genre and of the need for focus on key characters. Some sense of the varying demands of characterization might develop from such an exercise.

Eventually, students might be asked to systematize the methods of character revelation. One way to begin is to look at the sources of data on character. The nine possible sources for data are the three voices or speakers in fiction (the character himself, another character, and the author) and the three ways each of these voices can reveal some aspect of character (by something said, by an action or reaction, and by something thought). What students need to learn is that authors have these three "voices" and that each voice has these three ways of yielding character data. Students might take a very short story to begin investigation of these voices and ways. A story like "The Chaser" would do. Have a group of two or three students list every characteristic ascribed to Alan. Have another group list those ascribed to the old man. Once the character data is complete, questions might be asked about each piece. What voice—author or character—gives the data? How—saying, acting, thinking—does he give it?

Main characters in "The Chaser" reveal themselves mainly through *what* they say and *how* they say things. There is scarcely any revealing action; there is no revealed thought; there is very little author's description. The reader knows nothing about what Alan looks like but he knows everything about his naïveté: "'That is love!' cried Alan." Stubby Pringle is revealed primarily through his *actions*. Indeed, Stubby has relatively little to say. But what he does and how he does it in the several stages of the story give us his character and personality. In "Jacob" it is the narrator's *thoughts* (author-as-character here) that are primary characterization devices: the narrator thinks about the significance of the moccasins, about the meaning of childhood, about homesteading and other thematically relevant matters. So with Walter Mitty. The fantasies he creates in his mind are the full dimension of his escape from his wife-shrew and the society she represents.

Examples of revelation by "the other character" are also available. *What* Mrs. Wilson and Johnny say and *how* they say what they say to and about Boyd are the primary ways of characterizing Boyd: "Boyd will eat *anything*," Mrs. Wilson says. And "'After *you*, my dear Alphonse,' Johnny says. They began to giggle." Through such lines we get the easy, intimate relationship between the two boys and become aware of Mrs. Wilson's sense of Boyd as the stereotyped Negro. There is virtually no description in the story and very little revealing action. What each character says and how he says it are the bases for characterizations.

How do other characters' actions and thoughts operate to reveal Richard Pratt in "Taste"? It is Mike Schofield's competitive response to Pratt, the very fact that he wants to fool Pratt, that establishes Pratt's character. Mike wants to defeat Pratt on some telling ground: Pratt's knowledge of wines—and all the "culture" that knowledge implies. Mike's actions, his almost insane need to defeat Pratt (and thus "win" as a man of culture) reveal his thoughts —as "other character"—about Pratt; Mike's actions and thoughts are important markers of Pratt's character. Adding what we learn from Pratt's own actions (his gulping the Moselle, his repulsive attentions to Louise Schofield, his arrogance as he attempts to "guess" the claret) and from the author (Pratt's face that is "all mouth and lips," for example) we come to know and dislike Pratt. If we weren't to know him, "what happens" to Pratt would bring no pleasure, no satisfaction of plot appetite.

Distinctions among main characters' own actions and beliefs, and "other characters'" actions, statements, or beliefs are relatively easy to make. The ways the *author* makes character revelations are sometimes harder to pin down.

In "Taste," the author is *inside* the story, thinly disguised as the narrator-character "I." But even in third-person stories with the author clearly "outside" the story, what he thinks about what is going on and about his characters may be learned. The words he chooses to describe a character and the tone of the words he gives that character to speak reveal how the author views the character and what attitude he expects the reader to take toward that character. When Pratt smiles "a thick-lipped, wet-lipped smile," the author is telling us what kind of man he thinks Pratt is and is making sure we don't miss it.

Whether within the story (as the character "I") or outside it, what the author *does* to reveal character consists of what he chooses to tell, what details to include, which to magnify (such as the epithets Schaefer uses each time Stubby Pringle embarks on a new tack of action), and which to leave to the reader's imagination (the exact situation, for example, of the "old man" in "The Chaser"). An author's "outside" *thoughts* about a character, his "direct analyses," are sometimes called artistic lapses. (Until Wayne Booth's *The Rhetoric of Fiction* in 1961, it was fashionable to refer disparagingly to an author's "intrusions," even though our best authors have always "intruded," one way or another.) In order to avoid excessive intrusion, authors sometimes disguise themselves as the character "I" and narrate the story from within. The narrator in "Taste," a case in point, gives us the author's direct analysis of his characters. The student must learn that the way he feels about characters is ultimately controlled and determined by the author.

If identifying the voices and methods of character revelation is interesting and possible for students, more sophisticated questions might later be posed. For example, would use of a different voice have accomplished something very different in one particular instance? Would that "something different" have been more full or more effective? Is there a pattern in the way the author has revealed characters in a poetic story? How do the ways of revelation in one story compare and contrast with those in another?

Some exercise of characterizational method is necessary if students tend to dismiss characters like Mrs. Wilson in "After You, My Dear Alphonse" with a contemptuous "Stereotype!" She *is* that, but that is her function. Conversely, an overdrawn character in another story who doesn't function in developing the thematic or structural concerns of that story may destroy its unity. It is toward some such understanding about characters that we must move.

Point of view

Reducing abstraction. I've been in a junior-high class where an entire period went to discussion of differing points of view. If the teacher used the terms *third person* and *omniscient* once, she used them twenty times. And she used them once. Toward the end of the hour, the first student to volunteer a question asked, "Isn't point of view just another word for *opinion?*"

It was a good question, if untimely. The term *point of view* usually means "opinion" or "belief": "What's his point of view on that issue?" But arriving at the literary sense of the term might follow such lines as these:

You have read and discussed a first-person story; you plan to read a story (such as "Haircut") in which the narrator's view of action and character is critical. The term *point of view* has appeared on the chalkboard. "Let me see if I can get you to tell me what this term means," you say to your middle-track ninth-graders. "We want to learn something about *point of view* because it often determines the effect, the flavor, even the meaning of a story."

You select two students to present an impromptu argument between a father and his son. Each character is given four "facts" on which his position is based. For example:

"Facts" for father:

1. Your son hasn't had much driving experience; you've never let him drive alone at night.
2. Saturday night is the busiest night in town.
3. Young drivers are often careless or foolish.
4. The family car is new.

"Facts" for son:

1. There's a dance Saturday and you have a date.
2. You've had your license for three months.

3. Your father has said you could have the car for a date—
sometime.

4. You consider yourself a good, safe driver.

After the two boys have had a minute to consider their facts,
ask them to act out an argument between father and son. The argument begins after the son asks his father whether he can have the
car for a Saturday-night date.

When the argument has reached a conclusion or an impasse,
thank the "actors" and have them return to their seats.

It might at this point be appropriate to try to distinguish the
ordinary from the literary meaning of point of view. Start with the
common (nontechnical) meaning: "How did the father's point of
view or opinion differ from the son's?" Students will explain that
the son really felt he should be given the car for his date; yet there
were good reasons from the father's point of view why Saturday
night would be a bad night for the first solo flight.

Then you might say: "When you apply point of view to writing, it has a related but special meaning. Point of view in a short
story suggests where an author stands in telling his story. If you
were going to write a story based on the argument we saw, how
would you begin?"

Almost certainly students' first responses will be from the
"limited omniscient" view: "This boy had a date and wanted to
use the car, so he asked his father. But the father . . . ." Have a student begin the story from inside the skin of the boy, using the "I":

> Dad had said I might use the car sometime. When Jean said
> she'd go to the dance, I decided to start my campaign. After
> dinner I put on my best smile and hit Dad with the question.
> "Dad," I said, "I've got a date for Saturday and want to drive.
> Can I?"

I would settle for clarity and slight progress in this first exercise.
The key understanding is that where an author "stands" makes a
difference. Students will see that the author becomes a character
("named I") in the example above.

They should also see that the father could become the "I" character and that a very different story would emerge from that point
of view. Let them begin the story from the father's point of view.
They should be helped to see how the story would be different were
the "I" character a kind of submerged character—a mother, a friend
of the boy, a neighbor—witnessing the argument.

You might want to let them begin from a third-person point of view. In third person, "I" becomes a pronoun used only in dialogue:

> Jimmy found his father on the back porch. "I was looking for you," he said.
> "Well, you've found me," his father said. "What's up?"
> "I want to use the car Saturday night."

Whether these excursions conclude with the giving of such tags as first or third person is unimportant. That students see the differences among points of view is crucial. If you start with first-person beginnings, students should rehearse the obvious limitations of that view: the author is stuck with what his "I" character can see and hear; if "I" has to tell or know more than he can see or hear, another character will have to tell him things, or else the "I" will have to make some guesses: "I could see that Jimmy's old man was working up to a real sweat. His face didn't show much, but he started rubbing his neck with his right hand, massaging the old Adam's apple. I'd seen him doing that before and knew that it meant trouble." Students should sense the limitations of first-person point of view before trying to understand another point of view.

Other character "skins."   Have students review the feel and the limits of first-person narration. One student might be asked to tell what he has heard and seen since the beginning of the class hour. Questions follow: "Do you know what Frank is thinking? If you're not sure, can you guess what he might be thinking?"

The first-person story gets into the thoughts of others through such devices as "Mary seemed to think it was funny when . . ." or "I could see Manny didn't like to be teased." Ask the same students how, in a story, they might narrate what is happening "right this moment" in the principal's office. Show that the "I" must be informed somehow. The commonest way of informing an "I" is to have another character tell him something. "Mary came in from the principal's office and said that everybody there seemed pretty excited. A policeman was there."

Then have a student read a story beginning in which the point of view is clearly (if simple-mindedly) omniscient:

> It was right after dinner that Jimmy asked his father whether he could use the car.
> "Not on Saturday night," his father said, flatly. "There's too

much traffic on Saturdays." Remembering that he'd promised
Jimmy the car sometime, he smiled at his disappointed son.
"Sometime soon you can drive," he said. "But not Saturday
night."

At that moment Jean was telling her mother about her date
with Jimmy. "We're going to the dance first," she said, "and
then we'll drive out to Beth's house for scrambled eggs. Jimmy's
getting the car."

Help the students see where the author "stands" in this telling. Let them develop the rules for this point of view: the author
knows what is going on in each character's mind; he knows what
related things are happening wherever they are happening; and
so on. It might be useful to have a student provide yet another
demonstration.

Have him stand, assuming the omniscient point of view, and
describing what is happening "right now" in other classrooms,
telling what one of his classmates is thinking, relating this classmate's thoughts to an action or situation elsewhere. Once students
have been involved in "standing in different skins" as they tell or
speculate, application of perspective to material must follow. What
is important about point of view is not what it is called nor how
it is achieved. What matters is how point of view affects narration.

Students might next be given a new situation and then asked
to shape the telling through two (or more) points of view. Consider
this dilemma:

It is ten minutes before the annual band concert. For three
months the band has been practicing an original composition
by Mr. Kalin, the bandmaster. Four hundred parents and other
interested adults are waiting for the concert to begin.

Henry Scholz, the band's best trumpet player, has a terrible
head cold and can scarcely play. Since Mr. Kalin's composition
features trumpet solos, it looks as though the concert will flop.
Delbert Carr is willing to try the solos. Delbert plays second
trumpet and has attempted playing the solos once or twice.
Mr. Kalin knows that Delbert will try, but he also knows that
Delbert just isn't good enough to get through the piece without catastrophic mistakes. Delbert and Henry stand with
Mr. Kalin behind the curtain as the bandmaster wonders what
to do.

Eighth-graders could demonstrate understanding through
stories told from the first-person points of view of Mr. Kalin, Del-

bert, and Henry, and from the third-person and omniscient perspectives.

Does this seem a mighty slow business? The several approaches here fail to suggest how often, in how many different ways, a teacher must try to make concrete such abstractions as *point of view*.

The reader as writer: seeing short stories. Most rhetorical considerations, including point of view, align the reader with the writer. In reading rhetorically, the reader tries to read as the writer writes: he looks for rhythms and pace, for distances among characters, and he listens for the tones of dialogue and narration. J. D. Salinger's Buddy Glass tells us that true poets and painters are seers and that the crucial part of the seer's anatomy is his eyes. The author sees the action he creates, sees it both literally and figuratively; the reader who would "see" a story must see as nearly as possible what the writer sees. This kind of seeing takes point of view to its most fruitful end.

Aligning oneself with the author (playing author, in a sense) is difficult when the author seems to appear in his own story as a character. To consider this difficulty (and to illustrate what authorial role-playing involves), I refer to Marjorie Kinnan Rawlings' frequently anthologized "A Mother in Mannville."[8] In a Carolina mountain setting, near an orphanage, the narrator has rented a cabin in which she will "do some troublesome writing." In response to a request for a boy to cut firewood, the orphanage sends an undersized twelve-year-old. To the author-narrator's surprise, Jerry turns out to be an expert splitter of kindling. She grows extremely fond of him as she gets to know him. She is shocked to hear him say that his mother lives in nearby Mannville yet sees him only occasionally, but the narrator eventually gets over her annoyance with the "mother's" indifference to her own son. After all, the boy doesn't seem to mind: he's not lonely—"It was none of my concern." Before the narrator finally leaves for other parts of the world, for Mexico, for Alaska, then "heaven only knows what or where," she goes to the orphanage to attend to details and say good-bye to Jerry. But Jerry has gone off, neglecting his regular duties for the day, an irresponsible thing for the usually reliable little boy to do. Yet, in a way, Jerry's absence is a relief: the narrator will avoid the unhappiness of saying good-bye. At the end of the story, when she leaves money with an orphanage employee for a Christmas gift for Jerry, she discovers that he doesn't in fact have a mother.

8. I would be delighted if everyone unfamiliar with the story would find and read it. In deciding on priorities for the limited space available in this book, the wide availability of Rawlings' story argued against its inclusion.

Although the story is about the boy, we see little of him. Rather, his character is shaped for us by the narrator. At the outset, the narrator quotes Jerry as an authority on the setting. He speaks of the discomfort of the mountain winters and of the beauty of the springs. It is through him that the narrator knows these seasons, for she's there only a short time in the autumn. When Jerry is first seen, the narrator is absorbed in her work, distant. Her view of the boy is vague and unsatisfactory: he appears too small for the job she wants done. The reader becomes more fully aware of him as the narrator does, although it is still "offstage" rather than direct knowledge. Jerry is courteous and will not intrude while the narrator is working; his presence is noted more after he has left the cabin area than while he is in it.

In short, the narrator gives us two views of Jerry. In the "now" of the story, she is profoundly concerned with Jerry. But at the time of the action in which Jerry was involved, she saw him only fleetingly and cast him as a minor character who touched lightly on one episode in a life full of episodes. She accepts his courtesy and reserve as a convenience, an excuse to avoid an involvement she doesn't want. Jerry behaves in ways that relieve her of the need to be concerned—especially of his "mother's" neglect.

By the time the reader gets to the final episode, Jerry has been characterized twice: there is the Jerry of the Carolina setting—a casual, nice, vaguely disturbing, but essentially insignificant figure in the narrator's life; and there's the Jerry of the time of the narrator's writing—a time long after the episode has occurred. In this latter perspective, Jerry is remarkable for his integrity and self-reliance. The first view is given largely through fragmentary episodes, inferences, and comments on Jerry's characteristic actions. The second is presented undramatically as though an essayist were speaking directly to his reader.

To say that the story is told in first person is not to say much. This story could have been written from the third-person omniscient point of view just as well as in the first person. But the dual ordering of events and impressions through the narrator can be an exciting discovery for students. The juxtaposition of the narrator's experiencing events and, later, evaluating them—this and the timing of the final illuminating episode give the story life significance. The separation of the two views—the *then* and the *now* of Rawlings' binocular view—is active, meaningful reading. It involves both the content and the form of fiction.

Scenery. Nothing happens nowhere. The place of a story has to be described or evoked somehow in a reader's imagination.

Some description is concrete and sensuous—details brought into focus through their shapes and colors, through the sounds they make and the way they feel, smell, or taste. Individual details in a well-written story are often carefully patterned—enumerated in a sequence building up to the key detail, for example, or made vivid through a series of appropriate comparisons. Partly because our language is becoming increasingly metaphoric, comparison is more common than is concrete detail. To say that a giant redwood is four hundred feet tall and forty feet in diameter may be accurate but unrevealing; to see a character stepping back from the tree, craning to take it all in, and thinking of it as twice the size of the tallest grain elevator in St. Paul, Minnesota, may reveal the impression it makes on a specific character. The impression it makes is part of its description.

One of three basic things students should learn about the scenery of a story is that the author has made choices concerning what he decides to show and how he establishes his scenery; these choices determine how a reader pictures a scene. Describing a girl as "beautiful" or a character as "witty" says almost nothing. But specifics leave a concrete impression of a character. Pratt's lip, in Dahl's "Taste," might have been described as "delicately red," as "sweetly moist," and "sensuously full." But Dahl makes it "full," "wet," and "pendulous." Dahl's choices among words and comparisons make the lip a certain kind of lip and prepare us for Pratt's chicanery. Similarly, Schaefer's choices among possible details in "Jacob" help us to understand Jacob's character and to get what we are intended to get from the story. The narrator-as-boy plays at Indian fighting; he relates his father's attitude toward Indians: the only good Indian is a dead one. These juxtapositions supply the perspective that identify for us the boy's sympathy with Jacob and introduce an important dimension into the story.

The fact that an author has made choices invites us to consider, secondly, the quality of his choices. A good criterion for judging details is whether they yield the impression or feeling about a place that a particular story demands. In "The Chaser," we are told exactly what we need to know about the room in which the old man sells his mixtures—its size, furnishings, and general grubbiness. Just the right shop for the faceless old huckster. A feeling about place may be deliberately clouded to equal effect. Almost any story by Poe will serve as example here. In looking at details, the reader inevitably decides whether they work or fail in the particular story, whether the author's choices have helped or hindered his design.

A third thing students should understand is that setting and scene can be distinguished. Although nothing happens nowhere, some things can happen anywhere. Dahl's "Taste" has only a setting, a backdrop for trickery. The story could have "happened" anywhere—in the African desert during World War II, in a restaurant in Laramie, Wyoming, in an apartment in Brussels. What is essential is that the reader has access to the information on which the trick depends. It is the fact of the trick, not its setting, that is important. But Dahl's "The Landlady" cannot be pushed around so whimsically. There must be a fireside and a cozy home; the stuffed parrot and stuffed dog and that silent canary are essential in revealing the old lady; the primary fact of her character is that she kills and stuffs things—including young men. The irony of the coziness, juxtaposed against the dead things, participates in the telling of the story. They are part of its process and theme.

Students can develop sensitivity to setting and scene by remembering that an author has control over the details he presents, by examining the quality and appropriateness of those details, and by deciding whether they are backdrop to a developing plot or an integral part of it. The story in which scene is integral to the story is not necessarily superior to that cast against a static setting. About all we know about the barbershop in "Haircut" is that there is a spittoon, and that is enough: "Haircut" is a story about Jim Kendall's personality, and the story is developed, anecdotally, in settings outside the barbershop. But in a story where details are essential to characterization and theme, as in "The Landlady," perception of scene is seeing it work symbolically; that is, seeing it function to enlarge the story.

Scenery as symbol.   It is scene, not setting, that creates the tone, mood, and atmosphere that function as symbols in a story. Although the length of the short story often limits the use that can be made of natural symbols (the light and dark of day representing the good and evil in man) and private symbols (such as those that echo throughout a body of poems by Eliot, say, or Yeats), conventional and literary symbols are rather more common. By conventional symbols, I mean such things as the cross symbolizing redemption or love, or white clothing symbolizing the pure of heart. By literary symbols, I mean those that earn symbolic connotation in the context of a story, through the atmosphere and impressions they create. For example, a knife—outside the context of a particular story—is generally interpreted in Freudian terms. In a particular context, a knife might earn its own, and perhaps totally different, symbolic significance. Consider the knife in John Steinbeck's "Flight."

Pepé smiled sheepishly and stabbed at the ground with his knife to keep the blade sharp and free from rust. It was his inheritance, that knife, his father's knife. The long heavy blade folded back into the black handle. . . . The knife was with Pepé always, for it had been his father's knife.

Steinbeck makes amply clear that the knife evokes the thought of the dead father in Pepé's mind. And a symbol's function is to evoke. In "Flight," the knife has both concrete and nonliteral (or visible and invisible) meaning. To Pepé the knife means father, and as the story progresses it takes on additional meanings: manhood, suffering, death. The knife may be considered in a Freudian way here, if one wishes, but it earns its own particular meanings in the context of the story.

In Willa Cather's well-known "Paul's Case," to take another example, we learn in the first paragraph that Paul wears a carnation when he meets the faculty which demands his suspension from school. The teachers feel the flower does not reflect an appropriate contriteness of spirit "befitting a boy under the ban of suspension." Just before he kills himself, at the end of the story, Paul takes a carnation from his lapel, noting that the blossom droops in the cold, its glory past, and buries it in the snow. Between these two key references to carnations, it and other flowers appear in the story. To read the whole story, readers must come to grips with the significance of these flowers.

There is nothing obscure or mysterious in the knife or the flowers (or the symbolic journeys) in these two stories. It is not even necessary to label them "symbolic." But it is important that students learn to see and deal with the ways that objects, gestures, and patterns of comparisons both take on and provide richness within the contexts of particular stories.

Tracking down symbols is not an appropriate end in itself, but preparing students to consider symbolic connotation is simply good teaching: the preparation won't guarantee understanding of symbolic levels, but it will increase chances that many students will read beneath the top layer of a story. In assigning "Paul's Case," you might prepare students rather directly for what they will find: "When you first meet Paul in the story, he is wearing a carnation. He wears another carnation at the end of the story, and between these two occasions there are other allusions to flowers. Be ready to tell me tomorrow what Cather reveals about Paul through these references to flowers." You might first want to discuss generalized symbolic meanings of individual flowers—the lily, the rose, the orchid. But do this with an eye to dispelling the generalized meanings and getting to the particular meanings earned in the context of a particular story.

What's intrinsic / extrinsic?   Good school anthologies provide headnotes, illustrations, footnotes, glossaries, study hints, study questions, background essays, biographical sketches, exercises for improving reading skills, charts placing stories in their historical perspective, and other aids. These aids, usually carefully prepared and well-written, provide genuinely helpful introductions, questions, and procedures for teachers who literally cannot prepare every class hour as they would like to and as they should. But teaching aids—both in the anthologies and in the teacher's manual that accompany them—may be dangerous in their abundance. When an anthology's treasury of aids includes data that are not relevant to the stories they accompany, teachers understandably yield to teaching about literature rather than teaching literature itself. The issue for the teacher who does find time to prepare is: what is intrinsic to the story, and what is extrinsic.

That material is intrinsic which promotes understanding of the assumptions the characters make, or is built into the culture or scene from which the author writes. A student can hardly read Dos Passos or Fitzgerald satisfactorily without some knowledge of the ancient history of the 1920's—can hardly read *The Scarlet Letter* without some concept of the soul as a separate, enduring entity. On the other hand, great amounts of information—facts about the author, generalizations about the genre, speculations about which tradition the story fits into, and such—are likely to be extrinsic and irrelevant. Poe's emotional problems, Dickens' domestic relations, Irving's uneasiness in the new country, the quality of life on the Left Bank in post-World War I Paris, and such may be fascinating social or literary history, but knowledge of these provides slight illumination for particular stories. Yet too often, harassed teachers substitute such extrinsics for the intrinsic facts of literature.

Yet all kinds of facts—both in the story and outside it—are often necessary for full reading of a particular story. I've left some teacher's classrooms chagrined that a key bit of personal biography wasn't brought into discussion of a story. I've left other classrooms wondering (honestly, if ignorantly) what nugget lay buried under an avalanche of extrinsic data. There are two teaching questions here: what is the necessary proportion of text-based and extra-textual information for each individual story? And what is the best order in which to present the different kinds of data? I would like to say something wise and concrete about how to maintain proportion and balance in presentation, but I find myself capable only of this flabby generalization: insofar as background and contextual data contribute to a reader's ability to read a story well, it has value; moreover, relevant data should be presented at that moment when it has value.

The trick is to help the students make discoveries in the right order. First, we read with them what is set before their eyes and what is available to every reader, whatever his background—the text itself. Then, we invite comparison of things in the story with things we already know something of—our times, our problems, and so on. Next, we pose those intrinsic study questions (we may have to make these up ourselves) to be sure that the internal resonances of the story come through. Then, we place the texts we have read in the contexts of other works by that same author. Sometimes, we can set up echoes among works by other authors who practice in the same genre or who probe the same themes and materials. More rarely, we will bite into literary criticism and literary history.

Gossip about the author and other extrinsic information should be offered sparingly, and only when it illuminates something in the text. Focus in teaching the short story should be on the close reading of text. The teacher's lonely (but necessary) job is to decide what will be useful to students, and when. A case in point: "The Minister's Black Veil." In this story Hawthorne tells us that "once during Governor Belcher's administration, Mr. Hooper was appointed to preach the election sermon." Now, Belcher was Governor of Massachusetts from 1730 to 1741. Will it help students fit the story into time if they know this? Should they be sent to histories so they can "report back to the class on Belcher's Decade?" Should the teacher start out by trying to discover what students know about Puritan New England? Which study aids, which study questions will lead to a discovery of what is intrinsic to the story? Which will lead elsewhere?

Every question must be examined alone. Governor Belcher's administrative record is scarcely germane to the study of "The Minister's Black Veil." It is in the story that the Reverend Mr. Hooper wears his symbolic veil, not in the historical background. Conversely, some attempt to illuminate the meaning of the veil with outside questions is appropriate: do all men wear masks of some kind to hide their true natures? Do we accept the ordinary masks people wear every day? What kinds of masks might I have in mind? Such speculations can lead to the values that link Hawthorne's story to our very different time.

This complex story, whose time seems out-of-joint for the

sophisticated eleventh-grader, whose theme seems bleak and opaque for the unsophisticated, can lead some adolescents to increased understanding of themselves and their world. "The Minister's Black Veil" leaves us with things we know much of today: Mr. Hooper is a stern, authoritarian personality able to dominate large political and social groups; the generation of the story lives under a sense of doom, derived from fear of an angry God, but no less real than the doom derived from fear of The Bomb; the pieties, superficialities, hypocrisies, and terrible truths about human nature existed then as now; monomaniacal excess can still produce monsters who blight everything they touch, who destroy joy and cast a pall over love and make any kind of personal *human* relationship impossible. In Hooper's world natural depravity and original sin were powerful influences. Impotence and outrage and tragedy define Hawthorne's theme. Are they relevant to today's young readers? Both the college-bound youth and the academically disengaged are asked to read the story. *Can* they?

A few can, I think. Those who can will have to be concerned with the text and will have to have some sense of the context in which Hooper lives. But no student, particularly the disengaged, should be allowed to study Governor Belcher's administration in the pretense that he is studying the story. No student should be led to think that facts outside the story are the story itself. Close reading of a pastel magazine fiction would be better than fraudulent consideration of Hawthorne. If the central issues of "The Minister's Black Veil" can't be approached because the text is too dense, the story should be set aside.

When we select a story for teaching to an entire class, it should be generally accessible. We must try to help students discover what is there, but at the same time avoid telling students everything we know. Like the anthology's aids, those classroom notes from our college survey courses will tempt us. But to teach students to read as we have learned to read, we will have to ignore (artfully, selectively) much of what we know. We know, for example, that Darwinian, Marxist, Freudian, or certain unorthodox religious attitudes are reflected in works of certain authors. We must not fall into the temptation of reading particular stories as exemplification of such attitudes. Sometimes we will be able to get to those attitudes; sometimes we will be able to tell all we know. But to display all our wisdom at the outset is a mistake.

PART FIVE

Short Stories and the Library

The student who knows where and how to find short stories may be the student most likely to extend his reading in the genre. One conventional encouragement to additional reading is the teacher-prepared supplementary reading list, complete with bibliographic citation. Another is the setting up of a reserve collection either in the library or in the classroom. But superior to either of these is an arrangement that encourages students to become independent library patrons.

I believe in giving students a list of recommended stories, each with a brief annotation saying why the story is recommended, and asking them to select stories they are interested in and go find them. This exercise may or may not be tied into a class assignment. I would distribute with the list information on sources of short stories, sources of biographical and critical data on authors, and sources of basic locational indexes. But even with such information in hand, students will need instruction on how to use it.

A student who goes to the library to find short stories will probably first approach the card catalog. The catalog will tell him, under the subject heading SHORT STORIES, what collections the library has. The observant student will discover that many libraries do not shelve all short stories in a single place. Collections that contain the complete short stories of Edgar Allan Poe may be classified 808 with other short stories by American authors. Stories by contemporary writers, however, are more often treated as special collections, with the letters *SC* designating story collections. Other anthologies may be given the call number 390 and will be found in the classified section. (See p. 154 for reproductions of catalog cards.)

The card catalog is not likely to have cards for individual short stories. At one time libraries tried to enter title cards for short stories. This was a simple but expensive method of revealing the library's holdings. But in recent years, libraries have come to depend increasingly on indexes to short stories. The most useful of these, although not comprehensive, is *Short Story Index.* (See p. 155 for a reproduction of a page from *Short Story Index.*)

School libraries that do not have *Short Story Index* usually have the *Subject and Title Index to Short Stories for Children.* (Children's and school librarians helped choose the 372 books indexed.) It indexes collections useful from fourth grade through junior high school, so it is a good supplement to both *Short Story Index* and another valuable source, *Index to Fairy Tales, Myths, and Legends.* (See pp. 156-157 for reproductions of two pages from *Subject and Title Index to Short Stories for Children.*)

Because no short story index is complete, students should be encouraged to use the indexes in the collections themselves. Many libraries have their own special ways of analyzing short story collections, and students should be made aware of them.

Characteristically, short stories appear first in magazines and are then collected in anthologies. Sometimes an author's stories will appear in a single volume devoted to his works alone (*The Best Short Stories of O. Henry* or *The Collected Stories of Jack Schaefer,* for example). More often, different authors' works are collected in anthologies (*Modern Short Stories* or *Reading I've Liked,* for example). Many such collections of this kind are available in paperback. For a few dollars, students can acquire fine personal libraries of short stories. Each edition of *Paperbound Books in Print* contains entries for hundreds of volumes of short stories.

There are also annual collections of short stories of particular kinds. The Mystery Writers of America, for example, publish an annual volume of the best mystery short stories. The title varies from year to year. So does the title of the best science fiction short stories, published by *Galaxy* magazine. *Prize Stories: The O. Henry Awards* appears annually, published by Doubleday. Among the best known and most carefully selected volumes of this kind is the annual *The Best American Short Stories.* (See p. 158 for a reproduction of a page from this reference work.)

Students looking for information about specific authors can follow several leads. The card catalog may help; there may be articles about an author who interests them listed in *Readers' Guide to Periodical Literature*. The general encyclopedias, such as *Compton's* and *Encyclopedia Americana,* should be looked at. Many libraries collect information about authors in vertical files. And, of course, there are innumerable biographical dictionaries. One of the best for students is *More Junior Authors.* (See p. 159 for a reproduction of a page from *More Junior Authors.*)

Students should also be encouraged to read short stories in current magazines. Magazines such as *Seventeen* and *Saturday Evening Post* are obvious starters. Others such as *The New Yorker, Harper's,* and *Atlantic* can be introduced as additional sources of current short stories.

A limited number of short stories are indexed in *Readers' Guide to Periodical Literature.* However, this reference will be most useful to the student as an index to current articles *about* the short story and to reviews of books of short stories. Critical articles about writers are also indexed here. (A reproduction of a page from the *Readers' Guide* appears on p. 161.)

Study of short stories often results in students' trying to write their own stories. Articles indexed under the heading SHORT STORIES in *Readers' Guide* often contain "how-to-do-it" information, as do numerous handbooks on writing.

These are a few of the library sources available to the student. His study of the short story will be enriched if he will use them. If he does, he will have the satisfaction of discovery; and once familiar with such sources, he is likely to return to them.

Students looking for short stories collected by certain compilers will find cards like these. Although both collections contain short stories, their call numbers indicate they will be shelved in different places in the library.

Sometimes students can profit from scanning the list of contents, as given on the second card. They know that most books will also have title cards. The numbered markings on the bottom of the cards tell them which other subject headings the books may also be found under.

Although the card catalog is often the place at which students begin their library search, it offers little help in finding specific stories.

Call number

891.7
M889
         Compiler

Morton, Miriam, *comp.*
    A harvest of Russian children's literature. Edited, with introduction and commentary, by Miriam Morton. Foreword by Ruth Hill Viguers. Berkeley. University of California Press, 1967.

    xiv, 474 p. illus. (part col.) **28 cm.**
                                    Publisher and date

Other entries under which the book will be found

1. Children's literature (Collections)   ɪ. Title.

PZ5.M88Har   **j 891.7**   67–21384

Library of Congress   ᵣ3ᵢ

Call number

SC
R788s

Rosmond, Babette, *comp.*
Title of collection   Seventeen from Seventeen; an anthology of stories, selected by Babette Rosmond. New York, Macmillan ₍1967₎
    ix, 268 p. 21 cm.
    CONTENTS. — Uncle Hobey, by H. Fort. — Memento, memento, by M. J. Amft.—A snow statue, by R. Toney.—The gypsy student, by J. Schwartz.—The fairest hour, by N. Johnson.—The nothing box, by T. E. Brooks.—No boy. I'm a girl! By M. J. Amft.—The survivors, by P. W. Sullivan.—Catherine, by C. S. Gilbert.—Blue lawns, by P. Brodeur.—Where have you been all my life? By S. Lardner.—Mr. da V, by K. Reed.—A talent for delight, by P. D. Boles.—The ditch, by E. Bannister.—Little dog lost, by J. McCord.—The long ride to the city, by M. A. Carter.—Two nice girls, by F. G. Patton.
    1. Short stories.   ɪ. Seventeen.   ɪɪ. Title.

Titles of stories in the collection

PZ1.R718Se   67–17918

Library of Congress   ᵣ49–2ᵢ

Short Story Index, with its two supplements, indexes more than 75,000 short stories. Author, title, and subject entries are all found in a single alphabetical listing. The collections indexed are in a separate alphabetical listing.

All stories are entered under both author and title, with the main entry under the author's name. Many stories are also indexed under such headings as DETECTIVE STORIES, WESTERN STORIES, and SEA STORIES.

The student using the subject approach has three places to look to find complete information. The subject entry leads to the author entry, which leads to the index of collections. Title entries lead to author entries and then to the collections; author entries lead directly to the collections. Directions for use are contained at the beginning of the volume.

140　　　　**SHORT STORY INDEX**
SUPPLEMENT 1955-1958

IMAGINARY KINGDOMS—*Continued*
Howard, R. E. Shadows in Zamboula
Howard, R. E. A witch shall be born
Howard, R. E. and De Camp, L. S. The flame-knife
Howard, R. E. and De Camp, L. S. Hawks over Shem
Howard, R. E. and De Camp, L. S. Road of the eagles
IMAGINARY WARS AND BATTLES
Howard, R. E. Black colossus
Howard, R. E. Shadows in the moonlight
Howard, R. E. A witch shall be born
Howard, R. E. and De Camp, L. S. Blood-stained god
Howard, R. E. and De Camp, L. S. The flame-knife
Howard, R. E. and De Camp, L. S. Hawks over Shem
Howard, R. E. and De Camp, L. S. Road of the eagles
Howard, R. E. and De Camp, L. S. Tales of Conan; 4 stories
IMBECILES. See Feeble-minded; Idiocy
The **imbroglio.** Pincherle, A.
IMHOTEP
Cook, B. G. Egyptian fishing
Imitation general. Chamberlain, W.
IMITATIONS. See Impersonations
Immigrant. Simak, C. D.
IMMIGRANTS
Brackett, L. Other people
Schaefer, J. W. Man from far away
　　　See also French in the United States; Germans in the United States; etc.
Immortal bard. Asimov, I.
The **immortal** game. Anderson, P.
Immortal story. Blixen, K.
IMMORTALITY
Unamuno y Jugo, M. de. Saint Emanuel the Good, martyr
Unamuno y Jugo, M. de. Saint Manuel Bueno, martyr
Impact with the devil. Cogswell, T. R.
Impasse. Stegner, W. E.
Impatience. Sansom, W.
IMPERSONATIONS
Barry, J. Ice storm
Guilloux, L. Man's name
Maupassant, G. de. Rose
Munro, H. H. Schartz-Metterklume method
Queen, E. pseud. Lamp of God
Sherman, R. Barrow Street
Stewart, J. I. M. Grey's ghost
Stewart, J. I. M. Tom, Dick and Harry
West, J. Tom Wolfe's my name
Impolite sex. Maupassant, G. de
Important thing. Williams, T.
Important wish. Zimmerman, M.
The **impossible** he. Robinson, R. S.
Impossible murder. Lyon, M. D.
Impossible voyage home. Wallace, F. L.
Impostor. Dick, P. K.
IMPOSTORS. See Impersonations

IMPRESSMENT
Melville, H. Billy Budd, foretopman
　　　See also Shanghaiing
IMPROBABLE STORIES
Adams, A. Joe Jenks' pet ox
Campion, A. The centaur
Cunningham, W. Cloud puncher
Li Fu-yen. Man who became a fish
Pohl, F. What to do until the analyst comes
Steinbeck, J. Affair at 7, rue de M——
Tolvanen, E. Paper plague
Ward, L. L. Tobe Snow
Improbable success of Mr Owen Hood. Chesterton, G. K.
In a certain house. Jouve, P. J.
In a foreign city. Coates, R. M.
In a Jerusalem cafe. Agnon, S. J.
In a lane of Naples. Marotta, G.
In a railway carriage. Maupassant, G. de
In a small art gallery. Nagai, T.
In a spur of the county. Adams, A.
In an early winter. Angell, R.
In another country. Hemingway, E.
In haste. Rabinowitz, S.
In Hoka Signo Vinces. Anderson, P. and Dickson, G. R.
In Marburg. Barash, A.
In memory of John. James, D.
In memory of Judith Courtright. Caldwell, E.
In name only. Marlett, M. B. G.
In port. Maupassant, G. de
In St Valentine's church. Babel', I. E.
In screaming birth. Miller, M.
In sickness and in health. Gellhorn, M. E.
In the basement. Babel', I. E.
In the beginning. Gerchunoff, A.
In the beginning. Levinson, N.
In the blizzard. Lesiñs, K.
In the cemetery at Scutari. Sandoz, M. Y.
In the country. Maupassant, G. de
In the courtroom. Maupassant, G. de
In the eye of the storm. Fisher, D. F. C.
In the family. Mitchison, N. M. H.
In the French style. Shaw, I.
In the moonlight. Maupassant, G. de
In the morning sun. O'Hara, J.
In the other's shoes. Beauquey, M.
In the penal colony. Kafka, F.
In the ravine. Chekhov, A. P.
In the realm of terror. Blackwood, A.
In the spring. Maupassant, G. de　　s
In the subway. Khan, I. M.
In the time of demonstrations. Hall, J. B.
In the trenches. Barbudo, A. S.
In the wood. Maupassant, G. de
In the zoo. Stafford, J.
In Tripolitania. Pons, M.
In value deceived. Fyfe, H. B.

The aim of the *Subject and Title Index to Short Stories for Children* is to aid public and school librarians in locating stories on specific or related subjects, and in tracing hard-to-find stories.

Part I is a list of the books indexed, arranged alphabetically by the code letters assigned each book. The approximate grade level of the collections is given here. Part II, the subject index, and Part III, the list of stories indexed, are both in alphabetical arrangement. Many cross references are given to the more than 4000 short stories included.

Both the subject index and list of stories indexed lead directly to the collection desired. The code letters are so obviously abbreviations that Part I is very easy to use.

In 1915, Houghton Mifflin began a series of annual volumes, *The Best Short Stories*. Edward J. O'Brien was the founder of the anthology and served as its editor for many years. He was later joined by Martha Foley, who also edited alone for a time; David Burnett is now her co-editor. The editors, all capable literary judges, have compiled impressive volumes.

Although format varies somewhat, the volumes are primarily the text of the selected short stories, with brief biographies of their authors. Usually included are a list of distinctive short stories of the year and the addresses of American and Canadian magazines publishing short stories. In 1942, the series title was changed to *The Best American Short Stories*.

HENRY KREISEL

The Broken Globe

(FROM THE LITERARY REVIEW)

SINCE IT WAS Nick Solchuk who first told me about the opening in my field at the University of Alberta, I went up to see him as soon as I received word that I had been appointed. He lived in one of those old mansions in Pimlico that had once served as town houses for wealthy merchants and aristocrats, but now housed a less moneyed group of people — stenographers, students, and intellectuals of various kinds. He had studied at Cambridge and got his doctorate there and was now doing research at the Imperial College and rapidly establishing a reputation among the younger men for his work on problems which had to do with the curvature of the earth.

His room was on the third floor, and it was very cramped, but he refused to move because he could look out from his window and see the Thames and the steady flow of boats, and that gave him a sense of distance and of space also. Space, he said, was what he missed most in the crowded city. He referred to himself, nostalgically, as a prairie boy, and when he wanted to demonstrate what he meant by space he used to say that when a man stood and looked out across the open prairie, it was possible for him to believe that the earth was flat.

"So," he said, after I had told him my news, "you are going to teach French to prairie boys and girls. I congratulate you." Then he cocked his head to one side, and looked me over and said: "How are your ears?"

"My ears?" I said. "They're all right. Why?"

"Prepare yourself," he said. 'Prairie voices trying to speak

More Junior Authors is designed as a companion volume to Kunitz' and Haycraft's *The Junior Book of Authors*. In style and general format the book is like the many other Wilson Company biographical dictionaries. In alphabetical arrangement are contained biographical and auto-biographical sketches of 268 authors and illustrators of books for children and young people. Most persons represented here have become prominent since the publication of the second edition of *The Junior Book of Authors* in 1951. All of the sketches are informal and students usually find the autobiographical sketches especially interesting, as they do the many portraits included.

---

49   **Cleary**

MARCHETTE CHUTE

studied the history of England before we learned about George Washington. This is perhaps a good way to do it, since Washington was himself an Englishman, and this early training of mine may be one reason why so many of my books have English backgrounds.

I was especially interested in the first great English poet, Geoffrey Chaucer, and I specialized in his period, the Middle Ages, when I went to the University of Minnesota. Then, when I came to New York with my mother and sisters, I found the wonderful resources of the New York Public Library and decided I would like to write a story about Chaucer's England. The result was a love story for girls called *The Innocent Wayfaring*. Then I became equally interested in Shakespeare and his period and did several books on the subject. One of them was called *The Wonderful Winter* and tells the story of a boy who knew Shakespeare and acted in his company.

Over the years I have done seven books for grownups and seven for children. I illustrated some of them because I spent a year at the Minneapolis School of Art and know a little, although not much, about drawing. I like to do drawings, but I like writing much better.

I find New York a very pleasant place to live. There are fewer trees and rabbits in it but a great many more people. We live in

an apartment overlooking the East River, with gulls flying by the windows and a fine view of the new moon and the bridge and the midtown towers. Our balcony has a bird-feeding station on it, and a little yew tree, and the apartment is so full of plants that we might really be in the country after all.

Beverly Cleary

1916-

AUTHOR OF
Henry Huggins; Ellen Tebbits; Otis Spofford; Fifteen; Etc.

Autobiographical sketch of Beverly Cleary:

WHEN I was a little girl named Beverly Bunn, I lived on a beautiful farm in the town of Yamhill in the Willamette Valley in Oregon. Because Yamhill was too small to have a library of its own, my mother arranged to have the state library send out small collections of books. Once a week she acted as town librarian in a lodge hall upstairs over a bank. I remember how eagerly I waited for each new crate of books because I knew that a few children's books would be included.

When I was six years old we moved to Portland, where for the first time I had access to a public library. When I had learned to read, I made regular trips to the library. As I grew up, I read almost every book in the children's collection but I could rarely find what I wanted to read most of all. That was funny stories about ordinary American boys and girls. It seemed to me that all the children in books lived in foreign lands or were very rich or very poor or had adventures that could never happen to anyone I knew. I wanted to read about boys and girls who lived in the same kind of neighborhood I lived in and went to a school like the one I attended.

When I was in the sixth grade I wrote a story for my library class at school. The teacher liked it so much that she told me that when I grew up I should write stories for boys and girls. This seemed like such a good idea that I made up my mind that someday I would write books—the kind of books I wanted to read.

Readers' Guide to Periodical Literature is the basic index to current literature. Students familiar with its format and arrangement will have no difficulty in using the more specialized Wilson indexes, such as *Essay and General Literature Index* and *Biography Index*.

Sample entries are:
SHORT stories
   Let's build a story. E. S. Fox. Writer 77:17-20+ Mr '64

SHORT stories	Subject heading
Let's build a story	Title of article
E. S. Fox	Author
Writer	Title of magazine *(Writer)*
77	Volume number
17-20+	Page numbers, continued
Mr '64	Date (March 1964)

Twenty-three modern stories. ed. by B. Howes. Review Sat R 46:21+ Ap 13 '63 G. Hicks

Twenty-three modern stories	Title of book
ed. by B. Howes	Edited by B. Howes
Review	Article is review of this book
Sat R	Title of magazine *(Saturday Review)*
46	Volume number
21+	Page number, continued
Ap 13 '63	Date (April 13, 1963)
G. Hicks	Name of reviewer

An explanation of all abbreviations, signs, and symbols, is contained in the Preface.

See-also references lead the student to such headings as CHRISTMAS STORIES and DETECTIVE AND MYSTERY STORIES, where the student will find references to short stories themselves.